Infantry Conference Report of Committee on Organization: June 1946, Part 2

Communications, Infantry

The BiblioGov Project is an effort to expand awareness of the public documents and records of the U.S. Government via print publications. In broadening the public understanding of government and its work, an enlightened democracy can grow and prosper. Ranging from historic Congressional Bills to the most recent Budget of the United States Government, the BiblioGov Project spans a wealth of government information. These works are now made available through an environmentally friendly, print-on-demand basis, using only what is necessary to meet the required demands of an interested public. We invite you to learn of the records of the U.S. Government, heightening the knowledge and debate that can lead from such publications.

Included are the following Collections:

Budget of The United States Government
Presidential Documents
United States Code
Education Reports from ERIC
GAO Reports
History of Bills
House Rules and Manual
Public and Private Laws

Code of Federal Regulations
Congressional Documents
Economic Indicators
Federal Register
Government Manuals
House Journal
Privacy act Issuances
Statutes at Large

THE INFANTRY CONFERENCE

FORT BENNING, GEORGIA

R E P O R T   O F   C O M M I T T E E

O N   O R G A N I Z A T I O N

SHORT TITLE

MILITARY POLICE – INFANTRY REGIMENT

(O-2)

PRIORITY NUMBER

(1)

June 1946

ORGANIZATION OF THE COMMITTEE

Brigadier General Frederick McCabe   Chairman

Colonel William W. O'Conner, Infantry   Secretary

SUB-COMMITTEE PREPARING THE REPORT

Lieutenant Colonel John Williamson, Infantry   Chairman

Lieutenant Colonel E. D. Van Alstyne, Infantry

OTHER COMMITTEE MEMBERS

Colonel R. W. Zwicker, GSC (Infantry)

Colonel M. J. Young, Engineer

Colonel John T. O'Neill, Engineer

Colonel R. J. Meyer, Signal

Colonel J. A. Dabney, Infantry

Colonel Vennard Wilson, Cavalry

Colonel Bernard A. Byrne, Infantry

Lieutenant Colonel G. A. Nica, Ordnance

Lieutenant Colonel W. M. Summers, Infantry

Lieutenant Colonel D. A. King, Field Artillery

Lieutenant Colonel W. C. Chapman, Infantry

Lieutenant Colonel Carlyle F. McDannel, Infantry

Lieutenant Colonel Ellis W. Williamson, Infantry

Lieutenant Colonel Frank S. Holcombe, Infantry

Major William R. Lynch, Jr., Infantry

Major George S. Beatty, Jr., Infantry

Major Lawson E. Hann, Infantry

Major Edward W. McGregor, Infantry

Major Hunter M. Montgomery, Infantry

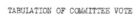

TABULATION OF COMMITTEE VOTE

RECOMMENDATIONS

	No. 1		No. 2	
	Yes	No	Yes	No
Brig. Gen. F. McCabe	x		x	
Col. V. Wilson	x		x	
Col. B. A. Byrne	x		x	
Col. R. W. Zwicker	x		x	
Col. M. J. Young	x		x	
Col. J. T. O'Neill	x		x	
Col. R. G. Meyer	x		x	
Col. J. A. Dabney	x		x	
Lt. Col. J. Williamson	x		x	
Lt. Col. E. D. Van Alstyne	x		x	
Lt. Col. E. W. Williamson	x		x	
Lt. Col. F. S. Holcombe	x		x	
Lt. Col. G. A. Nida	x		x	
Lt. Col. W. M. Summers	x		x	
Lt. Col. D. A. King	x		x	
Lt. Col. W. C. Chapman	x		x	
Lt. Col. C. F. McDannel	x		x	
Major E. W. McGregor	x		x	
Major H. M. Montgomery	x		x	
Major H. F. Crecelius	Sitting and voting with committee - Tactics "A" during this meeting.			
Major W. R. Lynch Jr.	x		x	
Major G. S. Beatty Jr.	x		x	
Major L. E. Hahn	x		x	
TOTALS	22		22	

THE INFANTRY CONFERENCE
FORT BENNING, GEORGIA

SUBJECT: Military Police--Infantry Regiment

    I. Papers accompanying

        1. Bibliography (Tab A)

        2. List of Charts (Tab B)

        3. Testimonials (Tab C)

        4. Extracts (Tab D)

        5. Minority Report (Tab E)

    II. The study presented

Should a military police unit be organic in the infantry regiment for the control of traffic, stragglers, prisoners, and displaced personnel? If so, what should be the general organization of this unit?

    III. Facts bearing on the study. (This question has been in conjunction with question O-7, Security Unit - Infantry Regimental Headquarters)

1. The infantry regiment is charged with traffic control within its area. (FM 7-40)

2. Whenever a regiment moves by road it has to post guides or road markers at road junctions, turns, and crossings to insure that no elements of the column become lost.

3. Prisoners must be escorted to the rear by the capturing units. Regiment should take over this job at battalion level so that front line troops are not lost to their companies for hours at a time escorting prisoners.

4. Combat experienced infantry regiments found it necessary to form a platoon in regimental headquarters, varying in strength from twenty-five to fifty men, and an officer. (Tab D) These platoons were called by various names; "MP Platoon", "Special Police Platoon", "Defense Platoon", and Security Detachments". They were used for any or all of the following missions:

a. Assist in establishment and displacement of regimental command posts.

b. Serve as guides and sentries at regimental command posts.

c. Act as security patrols to accompany higher commanders, regimental commanders, and/or staff officers on reconnaissance missions.

d. Serve as security force for the command posts.

e. Serve as trained route guides during tactical and non-tactical moves by the regiment.

f. Serve as prisoner of war escort from battalion to the division cage.

g. Establish traffic control posts forward of regimental command posts.

h. Assist in moving civilians from the regimental sector or zone of action.

5. The General Board, USFET, page 5, Study 15 recommends a platoon of one officer and thirty two (32) men for defense and MP duty be assigned organically to each regimental headquarters company. (Tab D)

6. Regimental command posts are likely objectives of enemy attack by aircraft, airborne troops, tanks, or infiltrating ground troops. Adequate full time security cannot be guaranteed by personnel or units having other primary functions.

7. Under present T/O and E there is no unit in the infantry regiment whose primary function it is to provide security to the regimental command post and do M.P. duties.

8. When the extra tasks of command post security, traffic control, handling of prisoners are met by using personnel with other primary duties, the effective fighting strength of the regiment is diminished.

9. Under present T/O and E (19-7-os, Change 2, 1 June 1945) the Military Police Platoon, Infantry Division, was increased to a company with strength of seven officers and 169 men. The basic elements of this company are one police platoon and three traffic platoons. Most divisions in combat reinforced their MP Platoons with additional personnel so that they approached or equalled a company in size. (Tab D) Despite this augmentation they were unable to help the regiments.

10. During the early part of the war regimental bands were used as defense platoons in regimental command posts. This procedure was unsatisfactory for it took bandsmen from their primary duty for long periods during which they were unable to practice. Casualties of three or four men from a band tends to seriously disrupt the band as a musical organization.

IV. Conclusions:

1. There is a need for an organic unit in the infantry regimental headquarters for military police duties.

2. Such a unit should also provide security for the regimental C.P. in combat.

3. The newly authorized division M.P. company cannot fulfill this need.

4. A regimental band, if authorized, should not be used for these duties.

V. Recommendations:

1. That a command post security and military police platoon be included as an organic element of the infantry regimental headquarters.

2. That this platoon have a strength of about one officer and thirty four enlisted men, with sufficient weapons and transportation to enable it to perform its duties. (See Chart in Tab B for suggested T/O & E)

VI. Concurrences

The committee concurs in the foregoing conclusion and recommendations (except for minority report as attached).

/s/ Frederick McCabe
FREDERICK McCABE
Brigadier General, U. S. A.
Chairman

BIBLIOGRAPHY

	TITLE	FILE	DATE	AUTHOR
1.	Report of General Board USFET Infantry Division	Study 15		USFET
2.	Report of General Board USFET Infantry Division, Question 14 App 3	Study 15		USFET
3.	Report of General Board USFET Infantry Division, Page 3	Study 15		USFET
4.	Report of General Board USFET Infantry Division, Section 24	Studies 102-106		USFET
5.	Military Police platoon organic in Infantry Reg't	Letter	1 Jan 45	George H Weems Brigadier Gen. James F Strain Captain, Inf.
6.	Traffic and Security Platoon	Obs Rpt	5 Oct 44	Hq. AGF
7.	Security Platoon Inf Regt		6 Jun 46	Hq. 4th Army
8.	Security Platoon Inf Regt	Letter	undated	Hq. 6th Army
9.	Regimental CP Security	RCT 180	20 Oct 43	Kirk A Meaders, Captain, Inf.
10.	MP Platoon in Regimental Hdqs.	Obs Rpt	21 Oct 44	Charles H Coates Colonel Inf
11.	Special Platoon	Obs Rpt	26 Sep 44	Meade J Dugas Lt Colonel GSC
14.	Comments F.A. School	Letter	28 May 46	General Hibbs
15.	Revision of T/O & E of an Infantry Regiment	Hq 319th Infantry	3 Oct 44	O L Davidson Colonel, Inf.
16.	Letter to Colonel Rogers	Letter	18 May 45	Col. A R C Sander, AGF Board.
17.	Band (Armored) Infantry Journal	Page 63	May 44	Warrant Officer Bandleader

TAB   A

The chart below shows a suggested organization for regimental military police and security platoon to be added to the Regimental Headquarters Company, T/O & E 7-12.

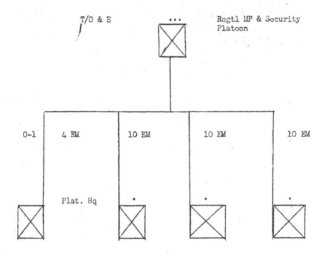

1-1st Lt Plat Comdr (CBN)

1-T/Sgt Plat (CBN)

3-T/5 Drivers, truck (R)

EACH SQUAD

1-S/Sgt Squad Ldr (R)

1-Sgt Asst " (R)

8-Pvts or Pfc Riflemen (R)

2-Carbines Cal. .30

3-Rifles Cal. . 30 M1

3-Launcher Grenade M7

1-MG HB Cal. . 50

2-Trucks $\frac{1}{4}$-t

2-Trailers $\frac{1}{4}$-t

1-Truck $2\frac{1}{2}$-t

10 Rifle, Cal. . 30 M1

3 Launcher Grenade M7

1 Launcher Rocket

TAB B

TESTIMONIAL

Major General William F. Dean, CG 44th Div.

I feel that it is necessary to have a small regimental M. P. Unit (about 1 officer and 20 EM). My experience was that each regimental commander organized one, even though at first I did not feel that it was necessary. I found, however, that such and organization for M. P. duty and C.P. security was needed.

Lt. Col. John Williamson, Infantry

Based upon my experience as regimental executive, Battalion Commander, and regimental commander in the 18th Infantry, 1st Infantry Division from 1942 to 1945 I believe a security and military police platoon in regimental headquarters to be absolutely essential. We used the regimental band for this purpose in Tunisia and Sicily but this was not satisfactory because the band had no opportunity for practice for months and it could not play for several days after we got out of the front lines. When the band was taken away from regiments we formed a so called M. P. platoon of an officer and 30 men. This platoon proved to be indispensible in handling POWs, taking them from battalions, handling them at regiment, and when necessary escorting them to the Division cage. It was also used as guides for road marches and for command post security.

Col. Stanley R. Larson, Infantry

Based on my experience as Commanding Officer of the 35th Infantry, 25th Inf. Div May 1944 to December 1945 I believe that a security element is necessary for regimental headquarters.

If, under the present organization, all personnel are used properly, there is insufficient means for a regimental headquarters to be defended against infiltration and small raiding parties. In the Pacific campaigns it was always necessary to improvise a bastard defence unit for local perimeter protection at night and it was a daily worry for the Regimental Hq. Co. C.O. to revamp his local

TAB C (Cont'd)

TAB C (Cont'd)

security arrangement because from day to day the number of men he had
to work with changed. Practically all enlisted men had to pull security
duty at night. - For short periods this would be acceptable to any
soldier but over extended periods, and for those men, such as radio
operators, wiremen, cooks, runners, mechanics, drivers, etc., it is
an excessive drain on one's physical and mental reserves to have to
spend half of each night on guard.

Whenever possible we used our I & R platoon for local security
but, as often as not, they were out on O.P. duty. On Luzon we had to
rely on the questionable capabilities of self-styled guerillas to
keep our Regimental perimeter safe at night.

At no time during the war did I ever feel that our security
was adequate, and I have often wondered if this serious oversight
(that of providing proper Reg. Hq. Security) would ever be corrected
in the T/O for the Inf. Reg. - Naturally, there are many other more
serious ommissions and deficiencies which should be corrected, too,
but this one cannot be overlooked.

My recommendation is that a re-inforced platoon (about 60
men) would be sufficiently strong enough to act as Reg. Hq. Security.
It should be equipped with BAR's or other light automatic weapons,
and M-1's. The automatic rifles should be in the ratio of 1 to 6 or
7 rifles because most of the firing by security elements is done at
night and at close ranges, needing wide dispersion to cover the
target which cannot be clearly seen.

The platoon should be equipped with a 60mm mortar, mainly to
be used for firing flares at night. Sniper scopes should be issued
to the platoon (1 to every 8 men) sufficient to allow overlap in
coverage by them.

This platoon could serve as the Regimental M.P. platoon,
functioning as such during the day when necessary or continuously
in rear and rest areas. Soldiers who have served well at the front
and deserve "light" duty for a change could keep this platoon filled
with battle seasoned and well respected men.

TAB C (Cont'd)

TAB C (Cont'd)

Just as so many other things are overlooked and quickly forgotten in peace which, in war, were critically needed, so will this little item of Regimental security be minimized and soon shelved, but in the next war our flexible T/O's will again be called on to permit us to reestablish our make-shift means of getting good security and having an M. P. establishment which logically can be a part of the Reg T/O.

TAB C

- 11 -

<u>E X T R A C T S</u>

A study of source material on this subject available (TAB "A") as well as personal reports from officers at the Infantry Conference shows that the following units either had or recommend a regimental security and M. P. Platoon.

1st Infantry Division			16	18	26	Infantry Regiments
3rd	"	"	7	15	30	"	"
84th	"	"	333	334	335	"	"
90th	"	"	358	359		"	"
102nd	"	"	405	406	407	"	"
45th	"	"	All Regiments				
80th	"	"	319			"	"
42nd	"	"	Recommends regimental security platoon.				
28th	"	"	109	110	112	"	"
35th	"	"	137	134	320	"	"
30th	"	"	117	119	120	"	"
34th	"	"	133	135	168	"	"
2nd	"	"	22				
44th	"	"	71	114	324	"	"
104th	"	"	413	414	415	"	"
87th	"	"	345	346	347	"	"
88th	"	"	349	350	351	"	"
91st	"	"	361	362		"	"
93rd	"	"	370	371		"	"
85th	"	"	337	338		"	"
92nd	"	"	365			"	"
83rd	"	"	330	329	331	"	"

Hq 5th Infantry Division - "Infantry Regiment needs security platoon."
Pacific Warfare Board reports that (7) seven regiments recommended a defense platoon for regimental headquarters.
5th Army Hqs. 28 Jan 1945 - "Platoon 20-25 is essential in each regiment for M. P. Traffic control, etc."

TAB D (Cont'd)

6th Army Hqs. recommends M. P. and security platoon.

4th Army Hqs. recommends M. P. and security platoon.

— — —

REPORT OF THE GENERAL BOARD UNITED STATES FORCES, EUROPEAN THEATER

"EXTRACT"

Study No. 15 - page 5 par 2d (1) (c)

No provisions were made in the tables of organization and
equipment of the infantry regiment for personnel to guard command
post installations, operate straggler lines, aid in processing of
prisoners of war, provide guides for making routes and control of
traffic. These jobs were of such importance that every infantry
regiment in the European Theater organized a military police platoon
to perform these functions. It has therefore been considered
necessary to recommend the addition of a military police platoon
consiting of one officer and 32 enlisted men.

— — —

Question 14 App 13 Study No. 15 in Report of General Board
United States Forces, European Theater.

Should a defense MP platoon be organic in the Infantry Regiment?

Major Generals	12 yes	:	4 no
Brig. Generals	7 yes	:	0 no
Colonels	19 yes	:	6 no
Lt. Colonels	9 yes	:	4 no
Combined totals	47 yes	:	14 no

TAB D

(Cont'd)

TAB D (Cont'd)

E X T R A C T

General Board Report USFET Study 15 Page 3.

(2) Military Police Platoon. "******The unanimous opinions of all combat
leaders is that the military police platoon is wholly inadequate to perform its mission, and should be increased to company size. Sorely
needed rifleman were used in every division to augment this platoon
during combat. A company has therefore been recommended".

SUBJECT: Observer Report, ETO

2 e. MP Platoon Organic in the Inf. Regt.

Military police platoons have been organized by detachment
of personnel from T/O units in the following organizations visited: 36th
Inf. Div; 9th Inf, 2d Inf Div; 22d Inf, 4th Inf Div. The following
comments were made by officers interviewed;

(1) "An MP platoon should be an organic part of an infantry
regiment. This regiment has drawn from rifle companies and has organized
a platoon of one (1) officer and twenty-six (26) men. Don't see how we
could get on without them, " - Regimental Commander, 9th Inf, 2d Div.

(2) "It would be exceedingly useful to have an MP platoon.
The proposed MP platoon should take over the security job at regimental
CP, be used for road markers and guides, handling P's etc.," - Regimental
Commander, 22d Infantry, 4th Division.

GEORGE H. WEEMS,
Brigadier General,
U. S. Army

JAMES F. STRAIN,
Colonel, Infantry

SECRET

TAB D
(Cont'd)

HEADQUARTERS ARMY GROUND FORCES

5 October 1944

SUBJECT: Observer Report, ETO, 11 Aug - 26 Sep 44.

4. Traffic and Security Platoon: A provisional police platoon was authorized by V Corps and 2nd Division to supplement regimental I&R platoon. It trained under S-2 and operated under S-1, S-3, or the headquarters commandant as follows:

> During Movement: Under S-1 (forward party commander) as route markers and traffic control section of forward party.
>
> During Active Operations: Under S-2 as PW escorts, PW collecting point guards, additional intelligence observers, gas sentinels, and camouflage guards.
>
> During Static Operations: Under headquarters commandant, as CP security, camouflage guards, and CP installation personnel. Squads of the platoon were employed individually on all missions listed above, singly and concurrently.
>
> Platoon consists of a platoon leader, a 2nd Lt., and three squads of one NCO, a sergeant, and five privates each. This personnel is carried on SD with regimental headquarters company from the several companies of the regiment.

— — —

HEADQUARTERS FOURTH ARMY
Fort Sam Houston, Texas

6 June 1946

k. Does the infantry regiment need a security platoon?

The Regimental headquarters needs security the same as any other headquarters and usually provides it.

RCT 180
In the Field
20 Oct 43

SUBJECT: Information on Infantry Weapons

Regimental CP Security

For CP Security, this Regiment uses the Regimental Band personnel. It is believed that defense platoon, added to Regimental Headquarters Company, could be organized and given specialized training in this type of security. Recommended strength of such a unit should be similar to rifle platoon, between 35 and 40 men, because many times the Regimental CP is right behind its leading rifle battalion.

KIRK A. MEADERS
Captain, Infantry
S-3

21 October 1944

SUBJECT: Interviews, Personal Observations, etc., in France
12 August - 15 September 1944.

1. e. Colonel R. G. Foster, C.O. 330th Inf, Dinard, 29 August 44:

"******There ought to be an M. P. platoon in headquarters company, 2 officers and 40 men, to take care of traffic, help with echelonment of command posts, guard prisoners of war and protect the CP.****"

/s/ Charles H. Coates
CHARLES H. COATES
Colonel, Infantry

SUBJECT: Observer Rpt, ETO, 13 Aug to 26 Sep 44

31 (1) (a) Add one special platoon with organization approximating
the following: 1 staff sergeant, 1 sergeant, 1 corporal and 30 PFCs or
privates - this platoon to furnish protection for the CP, guides, guards,
and men for other routine duties.

*　　　　　*　　　　　*　　　　　*

/s/ Meade J. Dugas
MEADE J. DUGAS
Lt. Col. GSC
Hq, 76th Inf Div

— — —

COMMENTS GENERAL HIBBS
COMDT FA SCHOOL
28 May 1946

The Infantry regiment should have a security platoon. As with
the division defense platoon, this unit can be composed of men who
through age or through minor physical disabilities are unable to stand
up under the hardships of field service with the rifle elements.

*　　　　　*　　　　　*

When large numbers of prisoners were captured during the recent
war, difficulty was always encountered in transporting and controlling
them. The augmentation of the military police company under recent
tables of organization will obviate some of these difficulties;
however, without setting up a large and cumbersome organization
which would be unprofitable, it is not felt that there is any
possibility of establishing, before the event, the means of
handling all the prisoners, which may be taken.

— — —

TAB D

Cont'd

HEADQUARTERS 319TH INFANTRY
Office of the Regimental Commander
APO #80 U. S. Army

3 October 1944

SUBJECT: Revision of T/O and T/E of an Infantry Regiment

1. a. Headquarters and Headquarters Company.

(7) Add a defense platoon consisting of one (1) Technical Sergeant, Platoon Sergeant; four (4) Staff Sergeants, Assistant Platoon Sergeant and three (3) Squad Leaders; three (3) Corporals, Assistant Squad Leaders; six (6) Privates First Class, and twenty-seven (27) Privates. Armament should consist of three (3) Rocket Launchers; three (3) Cal. .30 LMGs; three BARS; two (2) Cal. 50 MGs with ground AA mounts; five (5) carbines, and thirty-three (3) M-1 rifles. Two (2) 2-½ ton trucks should be provided to transport the platoon. This will permit the platoon to be divided and travel with the forward and rear CP's.

Primary purpose of the defense platoon is the defense of the CP installations. Secondary missions are: guards for regimental PWE, straggler control, emergency runners, traffic control, etc. Infantry regiment CP's are close enough to the front to require protection. It is impracticable to use present authorized headquarters company personnel or units detailed from other companies.

/s/ O. L. Davidson
O. L. DAVIDSON
Colonel, Infantry,
Commanding.

— — —

18 May 1945

Letter to Colonel Rogers,
G-2 AGF, from Colonel
A.R.C. Sander, member AGF
Board, MTO

Extract;

(Cont'd)

*   *   *   *   *

All regiments have a special platoon - guard, MP, traffic, PW
control, and CP defense. They chizzle it.

*   *   *   *   *

1025-45   2 7573

gp

Extract Infantry Journal, May 1944, page 63 by Warrant Officer Bandleader
Band (Armd)

Here is a brief note on what an armored outfit's band did
during the Tunisian Campaign.

Shortly after landing in Africa in December 1942 we stored our
instruments and joined the regimental service company and took over
duties as truck drivers and helpers. We then moved up to the scene of
action. Our job turned out to be that of hauling ammunition and gasoline
for the tanks, and rations and clothing for the men. We also got odd jobs
such as guard duty and manning machine guns for antiaircraft protection
in the bivouac area.

In the initial phase we lost four men, three of them key men
in the band-and-dance group, so you can see what a fix we were in when the
campaign was finished. We were happy to learn later that the men turned
up as prisoners in Germany and in good health.

We continued with the service company until the end of the
campaign. The band was cited by the company commander for the way in
which it had performed its duties.

After the shooting came a period of concerts and dances.
We built the band back to full strength, at that time twenty-eight
men, and were busy every day except Monday, which was the rest day for
the band. Believe me we needed that day of rest. Our day usually con-
sisted of morning rehearsal, a guard mount in the early afternoon, re-
treat, and finally two dances in the evening. Sandwiched in between
were occasional ceremonies such as evening parades and decoration
ceremonies.

TAB D CONT'D

But every rough lane has a turning, and finally we reached the turn in our long, long lane. Early in December 1943 we were told to organize the divisional band, using the two regimental bands as a nucleus and now we are in what might be said to be our seventh heaven. We have a fine concert band and three fine dance groups of twelve pieces each. Each dance group has its own show, the performers being the musicians themselves and you would be surprised at the amount of entertainment they put out. Most days we have two shows somewhere in the division area, and on an average of once a week and sometimes twice a week a band concert in one of the regimental areas in the division. We also go outside of the division to play at hospitals and leave areas.

For the first time in twenty-six years of service I can feel that I am doing a bandleader's job and I am thankful that I have a band that I can be proud of no matter where we play.

THE INFANTRY CONFERENCE
FORT BENNING, GEORGIA

15 June 1946

MEMORANDUM for Chairman, Committee on Organization.

SUBJECT: Minority Report No. 1.

The undersigned submits a minority report as follows:

1. Recommend that a band be a component part of any MP-Security unit that may be provided for the infantry regiment.

It is felt that:

a. A band is desirable for morale purposes.

b. A band whose sole mission is to play music, and which cannot have minor exposure to casualty is a luxury the unit cannot afford.

c. Immunity from danger and constant opportunity for practice is not essential to the quality of a band that can furnish entertainment as a primary mission and render ceremonial music as a secondary mission during combat.

2. In conclusion it is contended that soldiers prefer dance music to formal band music and that an available "pick up" orchestra, even though not highly proficient, is preferable to the occasional appearance of a formal band.

/s/ Bernard A. Byrne
BERNARD A. BYRNE
Colonel, Infantry

-22-

TAB E

THE INFANTRY CONFERENCE
FORT BENNING, GEORGIA

19 June 1946

APPENDIX 1.

CONFERENCE DISCUSSION

COMMITTEE REPORT PRESENTED

    O-2 Should a military police unit be organic in the infantry regiment for the control of traffic, stragglers, prisoners, and displaced personnel? If so, what should be the general organization of this unit?

DISCUSSION

    None.

APPENDIX 1.

THE INFANTRY CONFERENCE
FORT BENNING, GEORGIA

21 June, 1946

COMPILATION OF CONFERENCE VOTE

QUESTION: O-2 Should a military police unit be organic
in the infantry regiment for the control of traffic, stragglers,
prisoners, and displaced personnel? If so, what should be
the general organization of this unit?

RECOMMENDATIONS:

1. That a command post security and military police
platoon be included as an organic element of the infantry
regimental headquarters.

FOR	AGAINST
126	3

2. That this platoon have a strength of about one officer
and thirty four enlisted men, with sufficient weapons and
transportation to enable it to perform its duties. (See Chart
in Tab B for suggested T/O & E)

FOR	AGAINST
123	6

MINORITY REPORT NO. 1.

The undersigned submits a minority report as follows:

1. Recommend that a band be a component part of any
MP-Security unit that may be provided for the infantry regiment.

It is felt that:

a. A band is desirable for morale purposes.
b. A band whose sole mission is to play music,
and which cannot have minor exposure to casualty is a luxury the
unit cannot afford.
c. Immunity from danger and constant opportunity
for practice is not essential to the quality of a band that can
furnish entertainment as a primary mission and render ceremonial
music as a secondary mission during combat.

2. In conclusion it is contended that soldiers prefer
dance music to formal band music and that an available "pick up"
orchestra, even though not highly proficient, is preferable to the
occasional appearance of a formal band.

FOR: 17

/s/BERNARD A. BYRNE
/t/BERNARD A. BYRNE
Colonel, Infantry

THE INFANTRY CONFERENCE
FORT BENNING, GEORGIA

R E P O R T   O F   C O M M I T T E E
O N   O R G A N I Z A T I O N

SHORT TITLE

Graves Registration Unit-- Infantry Regiment

PRIORITY NUMBER
--5--

June 1946

ORGANIZATION OF THE COMMITTEE

Brigadier General Frederick McCabe	Chairman
Colonel William W. O'Connor, Infantry	Secretary

SUBCOMMITTEE PREPARING THE REPORT

Col. R. W. Zwicker, GSC (Inf)   Chairman

Col. M. J. Young, Engr

Col. J. T. O'Neill, Engr

Col. R. J. Meyer, Sig

Lt. Col. G. A. Nida, Ord

Lt. Col. W. M. Sommers, Inf

Lt. Col. D. A. King, FA

Maj. Herbert Crecelius, CWS

Maj. Lawson E. Hahn, Inf

Maj. William R. Lynch, Jr., Inf

OTHER COMMITTEE MEMBERS

Col. Vennard Wilson, Cav.

Col. B. C. Byrne, Inf

Col. J. A. Dabney, Inf

Lt. Col. John Williamson, Inf

Lt. Col. E. D. Van Alstyne, Inf

Lt. Col. Ellis W. Williamson, Inf

Lt. Col. Frank S. Holcombe, Inf

Lt. Col. W. C. Chapman, Inf

Lt. Col. Carlyle F. McDannel, Inf

Maj. Edward W. McGregor, Inf

Maj. Hunter M. Montgomery, Inf

Maj. George S. Beatty, Jr., Inf

TABULATION OF COMMITTEE VOTE

	No. 1		No. 2		No. 3		No. 4	
	Yes	No	Yes	No	Yes	No	Yes	No
Brig. Gen. F. McCabe	X		X		X		X	
Col. V. Wilson	X		X		X		X	
Col. B. A. Byrne	X		X		X		X	
Col. R. W. Zwicker	X		X		X		X	
Col. M. J. Young	Officer departed in compliance with orders prior to presentation of this study							
Col. J. T. O'Neill	X		X		X		X	
Col. R. G. Meyer	X		X		X		X	
Col. J. A. Dabney	X		X		X		X	
Lt. Col. J. Williamson	X		X		X		X	
Lt. Col. E. D. Van Alstyne	X		X		X		X	
Lt. Col. E. W. Williamson	X		X		X		X	
Lt. Col. F. S. Holcombe	X		X		X		X	
Lt. Col. G. A. Nida	X		X		X		X	
Lt. Col. W. M. Summers	X		X		X		X	
Lt. Col. D. A. King	X		X		X		X	
Lt. Col. W. C. Chapman	X		X		X		X	
Lt. Col. C. F. McDannel	X		X		X		X	
Major E. W. McGregor	X		X		X		X	
Major H. M. Montgomery	X		X		X		X	
Major H. F. Crecelius	Sitting and voting with Comm. Tactics "A" during this meeting.							
Major W. R. Lynch, Jr.	X		X		X		X	
Major G. S. Beatty, Jr.	X		X		X		X	
Major L. E. Hahn	X		X		X		X	
TOTALS	21		21		21		21	

THE INFANTRY CONFERENCE
THE INFANTRY SCHOOL
FORT BENNING, GEORGIA

SUBJECT: Graves Registration Unit—Infantry Regiment.

    I. Papers accompanying

        1. Bibliography (Tab A)

        2. Testimonials (Tab B)

        3. Extracts (Tab C)

        4. Minority Report (s)(Tab D)

    II. The Study Presented.

    Is there a need for a graves registration unit or a unit specifically for the evacuation of the dead within the regiment? If so, what should be the general organization of the unit?

    III. Facts Bearing on the Study.

    1. There is no provision in the Tables of Organization of the Division or lower units for graves registration personnel, or units.

    2. Reports from all theaters indicate that it was necessary for all units to provide graves registration personnel, and evacuation personnel. These units were organized within the regiment and invariably the rifle units supplied the personnel and equipment. All commanders expressed their satisfaction of the very high percentage of identification of the dead, due largely to the fact that the graves registration personnel were from the units concerned, and were consequently not only familiar with the battlefield area but the specific units engaged therein. All combat officers are unanimous in their opinion

that this service should not be furnished by combat troops.

3. The Quartermaster General, in addition to his other duties, is designated Chief, American Graves Registration Service, and is charged with the formulation of policies for its operation outside the continental limits of the United States.

4. The Army Quartermaster, as chief of the Grave Registration Service in the army, was charged with the execution of several principal Graves Registration Service Activities, two of which are directly concerned in this study:

a. Control of the technical functions of the Graves Registration Service in the army area, including the employment of Quartermaster Graves Registration companies.

b. Control of Evacuation of deceased personnel through the establishment of Graves Registration Collecting Points.

5. The QM Graves Registration company constitutes the principal agency through which the Graves Registration Service functions. The company collects, evacuates, and identifies battlefield dead. It collects personal effects and records and forwards them to the Graves Registration Division.

6. Graves Registration Companies were organized under Tables of Organization and Equipment 10-297. This table provides six officers and 119 enlisted men, including attached medical personnel. The company is divided into a company headquarters of two officers and 19 enlisted men and four platoons of one officer and twenty-two enlisted men each. The platoon is the basic work unit and is

designed to serve a division. Each platoon is divided into three sections with six enlisted men to a section.

The basic function of the Quartermaster Graves Registration Company as set forth in T/O 10-297 is to act in a _supervisory_ capacity.

7. T/O 10-298 provides for the organization of a Graves Registration Company that actually performs the _physical operation_ of the Graves Registration Service. This type of organization was not used during the war.

8. T/O 10-298 consists of four officers and 260 enlisted men including attached medical personnel. The company is divided into a company headquarters of two officers and 25 enlisted men and three platoons. Each platoon consists of one officer and 74 enlisted men. The platoon is the basic work unit designed to serve a division, and is divided into three sections. Each section collects, identifies, and evacuates battlefield dead. It is divided into a collecting squad and an evacuation squad.

9. T/O 10-500 provides organized graves registration teams to insure graves registration service for small forces, and these teams may be used to supplement existing graves registration facilities.

IV. <u>CONCLUSIONS</u>:

1. That responsibility for evacuation and collection are placed by doctrines and directives of the War Department and theater commanders. Actual method for accomplishing evacuation were to a great degree left to commanders concerned. In the absence

of any prescribed procedures there were varying
ideas among units as to how the job should be done.

2. That the removal of the body from the
battlefield is best accomplished by personnel
familiar with the battle area in order to obtain
maximum identification.

3. That though it is essential that
personnel of evacuating teams be familiar with
personnel of the units they serve, the use of
troops from units such as rifle companies cannot
be justified.

4. That the Graves Registration Company
organized under T/O 10-297 is inadequate to
perform the missions required of it.

5. That the Graves Registration Company
organized under T/O 10-298, with its responsibility
of physical operation on the battlefield has the
proper function, and adequate personnel to accomplish
its mission.

6. That it might be advisable to change the
name to Graves Registration and Collection Company,
in order to thoroughly emphasize the all important
phase of evacuation.

V. RECOMMENDATIONS:

It is recommended that:

1. A Graves Registration unit of approximately one Warrant Officer and five enlisted men be
an organic part of the infantry regiment.

2. The Graves Registration Company
organized under T/O 10-298 replace that organized
under T/O 10-297.

3. Higher headquarters recognize the necessity for the attachment of the QMGR Platoon to the infantry division, as authorized, prior to the divisions departure for the combat zone.

4. Division headquarters recognize its necessity for the attachment of the QMGR Section to the regiment, as authorized, prior to the regiments entry into combat.

VI . CONCURRENCES:

The committee concurs in the foregoing conclusions and recommendations.

/s/ FREDERICK MCCABE
Brigadier General, USA
Chairman

THE INFANTRY CONFERENCE
THE INFANTRY SCHOOL
FORT BENNING, GEORGIA

17 June 1946

SUBJECT: Question No. 0-3 - GRO

BIBLIOGRAPHY OF QUESTION 0-3
(Tab A)

1. Study of Reorganization of Service Elements, TIS, GNRIS-DN (400.34 18 Feb 46) General O'Daniel
   Inf. Conf. File F-14

2. Report No. 432, AGF Board, MTOUSA, 18 May 45
   Inf. Conf. File 1300

3. Immediate Report No. 117, Hq ETOUSA, 2 May 45
   Inf. Conf. File 1301

4. AGF Report No. 496 - Graves Registration -
   1 Jan 45
   Inf. Conf. File 1302

5. AGF Report No. 1065 - Graves Registration -
   29 June 45
   Inf Conf. File 1303.

6. Observers Notes on the Italian Campaign during the period 13 Dec 43 to 10 Mar 44, Hq AGF, Army War College, 2 May 44.

7. AGF Observer - Lt Col James C. Mott's Report on the Italian Campaign - 29 Dec 1943
   Inf. Comf. File 1306

9. Observers Notes on the Italian Campaign 4 Oct 43 to 29 Dec 43, Inclusive, Hq AGF, Army War College, 7 Feb 44
   Inf. Conf. File 1310

10. Overseas Observer Report, ETOUSA, period; 12 Aug - 2 Oct 44. Dated 16 Oct. 44, L H. Walker, Major GSC
    Inf. Conf. File 1311

11. Army Ground Forces Board, AFHQ - NATO, 26 Feb. 44
    Inf. Conf. File 1312

12. The General Board, United States Forces, European Theater, Study No. 107, File 321/9
    Inf. Conf. File 1313

13. Comments Commandant F. A. School General Higgs 28 May 46

Tab A

14. Studies and Recommendations by the Infantry School
    Code #18050   File F-1

15. Report No. 555, AGF Board, MTO 10 July 1945.

THE INFANTRY CONFERENCE
FORT BENNING, GEORGIA

SUBJECT: Question No. O-3 - GRO

TESTIMONIALS (TAB B)

LT COL W. H. SCHAEFER, Inf-

1. Based on my experience as C.O. of the 180th
Inf Regt, 45th Inf Div, I feel that grave registration
could be accomplished by a detail of approximately
5 men and a Chaplain. In the ETO, our unit did
this, and it proved successful.

2. I do not think that Infantryman should be
required to clear their own dead from the battlefield.
The result of this practice is a very poor morale
factor.

LT COL J. C. SPEEDIE, Inf -

1. Based on my experience as Bn Comdr in the
29th Inf for 10 months, I feel the grave registration
problem was not handled correctly.

2. There should be a specified grave registration
group or team on a Div level. In combat this team
could be attached to the attacking regiments and in
turn attached to the attacking elements of the regiment.

3. Both enemy and own dead should be cleared from
field of battle as quickly as possible. It is a very
poor morale factor for soldiers to view their own dead
lying in the vicinity.

4. I suggest that a consideration be made to use
men trained as morticians in some type of work in
graves registration.

-10-   Tab B

LT COL H. C. HICKS -

1. Based upon my experience as a battalion commander in the 16th Inf, 54th Regt, and Co. Hq, Special Troops, 1st Div, I feel we have a decided need for a better graves registration system.

2. Our unit had a detail of 2 or 3 men and a Chaplain. I believe a large unit should be provided. A company would be too large, however.

3. Failure of grave registration to remove the dead or removal of the dead by their fellow soldiers are both detrimental to the morale of the troops.

4. I believe it is a function of Corps, and sjould be accomplished by having a team attached to the Inf Division as Inf Regiment for the purpose of graves registration.

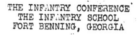

THE INFANTRY CONFERENCE
THE INFANTRY SCHOOL
FORT BENNING, GEORGIA

17 June 1946

SUBJECT: Question No. O-3 - GRO

EXTRACTS (TAB C)

1. Recommendations of The Infantry School, General
O'Daniel GNRIS-DW (400.34 18 Feb 46).

a. - - - In smaller units in general. Set
up: 4 teams in regiment, (1 regiment, 3 battalions),
total of 1 officer, 4 NCO's, 16 privates.

b. Letter from Col. Sanders, AGF Board MTO
to G-2 AGF, 18 May 45 - - - Several regiments have their
own graves registration section. 1 Officer and 3 enlisted
men, regimental section - - - . Most want a section in
the Infantry Registration.

2. Report No. 432, AGF Board, MTOUSA, 18 May 45
Sec. 8, Page 13 . We had to organize our own GR sections
in the regiment. The QM GR organization proved inadequate.
- - - I had one officer and 3 men in the regimental section;
one of the EM acted as records clerk. - - -
I think GR should be provided organically in the T/O & E
of the Infantry Regiment.

3. Immediate Report No. 117, HQ ETOUSA, 2 May 45.
Page 1, Par 4 "A graves registration officer should be
authorized in the table of organization of the infantry
regiment.

4. AGF Report No. 496 - Graves Registration, 1 Jan
45. Page 2, Par. 4 "Each regiment in this division has 1
officer, usually Asst S-1, Athletic and Recreation Officer, who
in addition to his other duties is a graves registration
officer.

-12-

Tab C

Page 2, Par. 6 (Div GR Report) - - -Army provided
a collecting point for us to turn over the bodies,
and this was the biggest improvement of all.

    5. AGF Report No. 1065 - Graves Registration,
29 June 45. Page 1, Par. 4. - - -Four of the six
divisions (ref: 76th, 78th, 87th, 102d Divs)
recommended that GR personnel be made organic in the
division - - - .

    6. From letter of Col. A. R. C. Sanders,
AGF Board MTO to Col. Rogers G-2 AGF, 18 May 45. - - -
Several regiments visited have own graves registration
section, 1 officer, 3 enlisted men. - - - Like it
better than QM. Wants Graves Registration Section
in Infantry Regiment.

    7. The General Board, United States Forces,
European Theater. File: 321/9, Study No. 107.
Page 4, Par. 9. " - - The company collects,
evacuates and identifies battlefield dead.
Page 6, Par 11a. " - - The general procedure
required combat units to evacuate to a division collecting point with the Graves Registration Service assuming
responsibility at that point.
Page 7, Par 11, a. 6. " - - 79th Inf. Division -
Members of the band were used for Graves Registration
Duty."
Page 8, Par 11 b. " - - However, evacuation by
Army and Corps troops was frequently direct to
cemeteries if conveniently located. - - - Corps
collecting points also received the dead from division
collecting points, thereby relieving the divisions of
the responsibility for evacuating to the cemetery."

Page 8, Par. 12a. "With the exception of the Third United States Army, the system of operating collecting points was generally the same in all Armies and subordinate units. - - - The method used by the Third Army in accomplishing the actual phase of collection, combined with evacuation is described as follows: - - - The assignment of a Graves Registration platoon to a division was found to be a waste of personnel - - - The problem was solved by operating one army cemetery and attaching a small collecting team to each division for the purpose of evacuating to the army cemetery.

Page 9, Par. 12 b 1. "Seventh Army - Normally, sufficient Graves Registration Companies were assigned to an Army so that one Graves Registration platoon could be attached to each division or task force."

Page 9, Par 12 b 2. "V. Corps (First Army) - Graves Registration platoons were attached to each of the three divisions of the Corps for operations only. In addition a QM service platoon was also "loaned". - - - The service personnel performed most of the essential labor."

Page 12, Par. 17. " - - - The system used by the Third United States Army of employing a small team from Army Graves Registration personnel to operate a division collecting point and other small teams to evacuate from such points is believed sound and workable - - - ."

Page 45, Par. 52. "Conclusions. - - - That evacuation

and collection of deceased personnel are best
accomplished by trained teams serving with combat
units. Teams should be organic to or attached to
units the size of regimental combat teams or combat
commands.

8. Comments General Hibbs - Commandant F. A.
School 28 May 46. "A graves registration unit
should be organic to the infantry regiment. It
should be placed in the service company and should
operate with the graves registration unit suggested
above for inclusion in the QM Company."

THE INFANTRY CONFERENCE
FORT BENNING, GEORGIA

21 June 1946

APPENDIX 1.

CONFERENCE DISCUSSION

COMMITTEE REPORT PRESENTED

O-3 Is there a need for a graves registration unit or a
unit specifically for the evacuation of the dead within the
regiment? If so, what should be the general organization of
this unit?

DISCUSSION

None

THE INFANTRY CONFERENCE
FORT BENNING, GEORGIA

21 June 1946

QUESTION O-3 "Is there a need for a graves registration unit or a unit
    specifically for the evacuation of the dead within the regiment? If so
    what should be the general organization of the unit?

RECOMMENDATIONS:

   1. A Graves Reistration unit of approximately one Warrant Officer
        and five enlisted men be an organic part of the infantry regiment.

             FOR 122   AGAINST 1

   2. The Graves Registration Company organized under T/O 10-298 replace
        that organized under T/O 10-297.

             FOR 221   AGAINST 0

   3. Higher headquarters recognize the necessity for the attachment of
        the QMGR Platoon to the infantry division, as authorized, prior to
        the divisions departure for the combat zone.

             FOR 123   AGAINST 0

Cavalry Reconnaissance Troop — Infantry Division

THE INFANTRY CONFERENCE
FORT BENNING, GEORGIA

R E P O R T   O F   C O M M I T T E E
O N   O R G A N I Z A T I O N

SHORT TITLE
CAVALRY RECONNAISSANCE TROOP—INFANTRY DIVISION
(O-4)

PRIORITY NUMBER
(8)

June 1946

ORGANIZATION OF THE COMMITTEE

Brigadier General Frederick McCabe	Chairman
Colonel William W. O'Connor, Infantry	Secretary

SUBCOMMITTEE PREPARING THE REPORT

Colonel Vennard Wilson, Cavalry	Chairman

Colonel Bernard A. Byrne, Infantry

Lieutenant Colonel Ellis W. Williamson, Infantry

Lieutenant Colonel Frank S. Holcombe, Infantry

Major Edward W. McGregor, Infantry

Major Hunter M. Montgomery, Infantry

OTHER COMMITTEE MEMBERS

Colonel R. W. Zwicker, GSC (Infantry)

Colonel M. J. Young, Engineer

Colonel John T. O'Neill, Engineer

Colonel R. J. Meyer, Signal

Colonel J. A. Dabney, Infantry

Lieutenant Colonel John Williamson, Infantry

Lieutenant Colonel E. D. Van Alstyne, Infantry

Lieutenant Colonel G. A. Nida, Ordnance

Lieutenant Colonel W. M. Summers, Infantry

Lieutenant Colonel D. A. King, Field Artillery

Lieutenant Colonel W. C. Chapman, Infantry

Lieutenant Colonel Carlyle F. McDannel, Infantry

Major Herbert F. Crecelius, Chemical Warfare Service

Major William R. Lynch, Jr., Infantry

Major George S. Beatty, Jr., Infantry

Major Lawson E. Hahn, Infantry

TABULATION OF COMMITTEE VOTE

RECOMMENDATIONS

	No. 1		No.		No.		No.		No.		No.		No.	
	Yes	No	Yes	No	Yes	No	Yes	No	Yes	No	Yes	No	Yes	No
Brig Gen F. McCabe	X													
Col V. Wilson	X													
Col B. A. Byrne	X													
Col R. W. Zwicker	X													
Col M. J. Young	X													
Col J. T. O'Neill	X													
Col R. J. Meyer	X													
Col J. A. Dabney	X													
Lt Col J. Williamson	X													
Lt Col E. D. VanAlstyne	X													
Lt Col E. W. Williamson	X													
Lt Col F. S. Holcombe	X													
Lt Col G. A. Nida	X													
Lt Col W. M. Summers	X													
Lt Col D. A. King	X													
Lt Col W. C. Chapman	X													
Lt Col C. F. McDannel	X													
Major E. W. McGregor	X													
Major H. M. Montgomery	X													
Major H. F. Crecelius	Sitting and voting with Comm Tactics 'A' during this meeting.													
Major W. R. Lynch Jr	X													
Major G. S. Beatty Jr	X													
Major L. E. Hahn	X													
TOTALS	22	0												

THE INFANTRY-CONFERENCE

Fort Benning, Georgia

17 June 1946

SUBJECT: Cavalry Reconnaissance Troop-Infantry Division

I.   Papers accompanying.

    1. Bibliography (Tab A)

    2. List of Charts (Tab B)

    3. Testimonal (Tab C)

    4. Extracts (Tab D)

II.   The study presented.

Is the Cavalry Reconnaissance Troop of the infantry division adequate as currently organized? If not, what general changes are desired?

III. Facts bearing on the study.

1. Of the infantry divisions employed during the campaign of Western Europe the great majority report that the Cavalry Reconnaissance Troop does not have sufficient personnel and armament to force reconnaissance or to carry out sustained battle reconnaissance.

2. Tanks, tank destroyers, and artillery have frequently been attached to the Cavalry Reconnaissance Troops as added reinforcements to enable them to carry out their assigned missions.

3. Lack of dismounted strength made this unit roadbound and unable to carry out detailed ground reconnaissance in keeping with the needs of the infantry division.

4. The area of operations of a division is sufficiently small that no great problem of gasoline supply would be caused if the reconnaissance troop used light tanks instead of wheeled armored vehicles.

5. In considering the possible organizations to replace the present division reconnaissance unit, the following types were investigated:

a. The new Armored Cavalry Troop of the Armored Cavalry Squadron, as recommended by the Armored Conference in May 1946. Troop strength approximately 200.

b. A squadron composed of two of the above troops, strength approximately 500.

c. A squadron composed of three of the above troops, strength approximately 750.

d. For a description of the Armored Cavalry Troop mentioned above see Tab B. It consists essentially of a headquarters and three reconnaissance platoons.

Each platoon consists of 2 O's and 49 EM as below:

(1) 2 mounted Rcn sections, 20 men, 2 light tanks M24, 4 trucks ¼-ton.

(2) Plat Hq, 1 O.,2 EM, 1 truck ¼-ton.

(3) Dismtd Rcn section, 1 O, 23 EM, 2 personnel carriers.

(4) 1 support weapon, (81mm mortar or 75mm Recoilless Rifle), 4 EM, 2 truck ¼-ton.

IV. Conclusions.

The cavalry reconnaissance troop of the infantry division as presently organized and equipped cannot accomplish the missions required of it because of the lack of proper vehicles, and the insufficiency of dismounted rifle strength.

The Armored Cavalry Troop approved at the Armored Conference in May 1946 does provide adequate tank strength and dismounted rifle strength. It is suitable for use in the infantry division.

V. Recommendations.

It is recommended that the cavalry reconnaissance troop authorized by current T/O & E for the infantry division be replaced by an armored cavalry troop of approximate strength of 200, and organized in general along the lines of that shown in Tab B.

VI. The committee concurs in the foregoing conclusions and recommendations.

FREDERICK McCABE
Brigadier General, U.S.A.
Chairman

4

TAB A

BIBLIOGRAPHY

	TITLE	CODE NO.	FILE NO.	DATE	AUTHOR
1.	Report - AGF Board MTO - No. A-593	G2-AGF	A-593	6 Jul 45	E.M.Almond,Maj Gen 92d Div
2.	Report No. 72, AGF Board,AFHQ-NATO Incl #9	G2-AGF	1-0932	8 Nov 43	K.E.Rice,Capt,Rcn Tr, 34th Div
3.	AGF Board Report -ETO- "Miscellaneous Infantry"			13 May 45	Maj Gen Wyman, CG 71st Div
4.	Observer's Report, ETO 12 Aug 44 - 10 Oct 44			21 Oct 44	E.J.Leary,Lt Col GSC Hq 69 Inf Div
5.	Observer's Interview with Ex O, Rcn Tr, 45th Div			17 Oct 43	1st Lt Ruhmann, Rcn Tr, 45th Div
6.	Report - AGF Board - NATO No. 125			18 Jan 44	Lt Col Reichman, G-2 45th Div
7.	Observer's Report Okinawa Operation			1 May 45	W.N.Todd,Jr.,Col., Cav.
8.	Unit History, 45th Cav Rcn Tr, NATO	D 809.53 .45th .A 2	17922	May-Sept 43	
9.	Report,AGF Board MTO No. A-424	D 731.1 N 51 #424 Res	2-8236	29 Mar 45	E.M.Almond,Maj Gen 92d Div
10.	Comments, Comdt FA School		Ltr	28 May 46	Gen Hibbs
11.	Comments, Comdt Cav School		Ltr	31 May 46	Comdt Cav School
12.	Observer's Report, ETO	G-2-AGF	20196	21 Oct 44	E.J.Leary,Lt Col GSC, 69 Inf Div
13.	Report,AGF Board, AFHQ-NATO-No 76 Inclosure No. 2, "Recommendations for Rcn Tr."	G2-AGF	(A-76-2)	14 Nov 43	Capt Flanders, 45th Cav Rcn Tr
14.	Reports from AGF Board Col Hamilton's Interview Regarding Rcn Tr 45th Div	G2-AGF	025384	2 Aug 43	Capt Flanders,45th Cav Rcn Tr
15.	Report, AGF Board AFH Q-NATO- No 86	G2-AGF (A-86)	95840	1 Dec 43	N.P.Morrow,Col FA
16.	Report, General Board U.S.Forces, ETO Study No. 15	320.2/9	No. 15	Dec 45	

TAB A

BIBLIOGRAPHY

TITLE	CODE NO.	FILE NO.	DATE	AUTHOR
17. Report, General Board, U.S.Forces, ETO, Study #17			Dec 45	
18. Comments Hq 4th Army			6 Jun 46	
19. Report of First Army Infantry Conference			6 Jun 46	
20. Report Hq Eighth Army			9 May 46	R.L.Eichelberger Lt Gen.CG 8th Army

TAB 4

ARMORED CAVALRY RECONNAISSANCE PLATOON

Recommended at Armored Conference
May 1946
Strength 2-0,   49 EM

| 3 | 3 | ¼ ton | Cal. 30 Mounted Reconnaissance
20 EM |

| 3 | 3 | ¼ ton | Cal. 50   2 Sections |

| 4 | 4 | Armored Vehicle
May be either
Light Tank M24 - 75mm
Armored Car M8 - 37mm
New Armored Vehicle - 75mm |

| 1-2 | ¼ ton | | Platoon Headquarters
1-0   2 EM |

| 1-11 | 12 | Armored
Personnel
Carrier
Cal. 50 | Dismounted Reconnaiss-
1-0   23 EM ance |

| | ¼ ton with
81 mm Mortar
or
75 mm Rifle | Support Weapon
4 EM |

| | ¼ ton w/trailer
Ammunition |

Armored Cavalry Troop

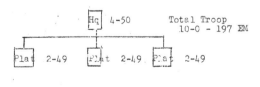

Hq 4-50   Total Troop
10-0 - 197 EM

Plat 2-49   Plat 2-49   Plat 2-49

TAB C

T..e following questionnaire was answered by members present at the Infantry Conference. A tabulation of votes has been inserted.

It is generally agreed that the division reconnaissance troop is not sufficiently strong for its missions. Its present strength is approximately 135 EM.

1. Would a troop of approximately 200 strength containing light tanks and additional rifle strength be satisfactory? (This is the new cavalry troop approved at the Ar...red Conference.)

YES 16   NO 3

2. Is a squadron preferable to a troop?

YES 4   NO 15

3. If a squadron is desired, should it contain:

    (a) 2 Rcn troops (strength approximately 500)? - (2 votes)
    (b) 3 Rcn troops (strength approximately 750)? - (1 vote)
    (c) 3 Rcn troops, supported by tank troops, rifle troop,
        assault gun troop. (Full squadron as used in corp
        cavalry. Strength approximately 1100)?

4. Should cavalry title designation be changed to infantry, and should personnel be infantry?

*YES 10   NO 10

5. Do you consider that the attachment of a platoon from the Div Rcn unit when required by regiments would eliminate the need for the regimental I & R platoon?

YES 1   NO 20

V. WILSON
Col, Cav

* After discussion and consideration of question number four, the committee on organization voted 18 to 1 in favor of retaining cavalry personnel in the reconnaissance unit.

8

TAB D

EXTRACTS

1. Extract of Study #17 by the General Board, United States Forces, European Theater on the subject, "Types of Divisions -- Post-War Army," dated December, 1945.

"......In its conduct of close battle reconnaissance, in its fight for information and in its screening operations during rapid movement, the (reconnaissance) troop was handicapped in many ways. It possessed insufficient dismounted strength and its main fighting vehicles were under-armored and under-gunned........."

2. Extract of AGF Report No. 941, "Miscellaneous Infantry," dated 13 May 1945 -- Comments of Major General Wyman, Commanding 71st Division. "The reconnaissance troop of the infantry division cannot accomplish the missions required because of lack of strength and punch......."

3. Extract of Observer's Report, ETO, 12 August 1944 - 10 Oct 1944 (Lt Col E. J. Leary, GSC).

"......It is generally believed the division reconnaissance troop as now organized has neither sufficient personnel for satisfactory reconnaissance nor adequate equipment to do a fighting job. In the 9th Division the troop has been used for both purposes. On one occasion this small unit was assigned a screening mission on a front 15 miles wide. ...... As presently constituted the troop is roadbound and the principal missions assigned to it are to reconnoiter and patrol roads, precede the division on marches and reconnoiter flanks."

4. Extract of Findings of First Army Infantry Conference, 2 June - 6 June, 1946.

"The Infantry Division Cavalry Reconnaissance Troop is not adequate as currently organized. ...... The reconnaissance troop should be reorganized to increase the rifle personnel available for dismounted action in each reconnaissance platoon. The armored cars in the troop should be replaced by M24 light tanks as an interim measure until a suitable armored reconnaissance vehicle is developed. ...."

5. Extract of Study #15 by The General Board, United States Forces, European Theater on the subject, "Organization, Equipment and Tactical Employment of the Infantry Division," dated December 1945.

".....The cavalry reconnaissance troop, mechanized, infantry division is the mobile reconnaissance element available to the division commander. Of the reconnaissance missions performed during combat, the majority were battle reconnaissance or reconnaissance in force. However, the troop had insufficient strength to accomplish desired results. Many divisions were reinforced by the attachment of cavalry squadrons to perform the intelligence and counterintelligence missions required. A unit to gain information under the direct control of the division commander is essential. However, the unit so employed must have sufficient strength, speed, mobility, and fire power to contact the enemy, obtain desired information and report that information to the commanding general. Armor and sufficient fire power are lacking in the present reconnaissance troop. ...."

6. Extract of Army Ground Forces Board Report on the subject, "Reconnaissance Unit (Division)," dated 18 January 1944 (Lt Col Reichman, G-2, 45th Div).

"The Reconnaissance Troop is not adequate in strength or equipment. ......The present troop is never strong enough to push back a German rear-guard, which always has both armor and AT guns. Also the present troop can't cover enough front. The troop functioned well.... after it had a light tank company attached to it......."

7. Extract of Comments by General Hibbs, Comdt FA School, dated 28 May 1946.

"The cavalry mechanized troop is inadequate. It is suggested that the size of the unit be increased...... With the increasing possibility of the use of air-transported troops of one variety or another in combat, it is highly desirable to have a mobile unit which can be used to patrol rear areas, to establish rear OPs, and to strike with armored fire power should paratroops or other airborne units land in the division area.

The equipment provided the cavalry mechanized troop is inadequate;
it is suggested that the scout car be eliminated and replaced by some
type of light tank. .....

8. Extract of Comments by Lt Gen R. L. Eichelberger, CG, 8th Army,
dated 9 May 1946.

"It is believed that the Division Reconnaissance Troop as
currently organized is adequate. It is impracticable for a T/O to meet
all requirements of varied terrain in different theaters. In the
Pacific Theater, in general the roadnet and bridge capacities as well
as jungle conditions limited the use of heavy reconnaissance vehicles
and made it necessary to utilize lighter vehicles. It is not considered
necessary to increase the grade of the troop commander to that of major."

THE INFANTRY CONFERENCE
FORT BENNING, GEORGIA

20 June 1946.

APPENDIX 1.

CONFERENCE DISCUSSION

COMMITTEE REPORT PRESENTED

O-4 Is the cavalry reconnaissance troop of the infantry
division adequate as currently organized? If not, what general
changes are desired?

DISCUSSION

Lt. Colonel R. E. Moore, Army Ground Force Board No. 2.

Recommend the deletion of the words, "Armored Cavalry Troops,"
and substitute therefor, "Infantry Reconnaissance Company."

Colonel John Dabney, Hq., Army Ground Forces.

My purpose—my remarks for saying that I am a Doughboy. Until
such time as we do away with arm or brass distinction entirely,
I don't believe the proposal to make this troop infantry is
sound. A division is still a force of combined arms and one of
the primary missions of armored cavalry is reconnaissance. We
might as well say that we would make the infantry of the Armored
Division, armor, as to say that we would make this cavalry troop,
infantry. I would support the stand that we leave it, "Armored
Cavalry."

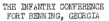

THE INFANTRY CONFERENCE
FORT BENNING, GEORGIA

21 June 1946

COMPILATION OF CONFERENCE VOTER

QUESTION: O-4. Is the Cavalry Reconnaissance Troop of the Infantry Division adequate as currently organized? If not, what general changes are desired?

RECOMMENDATIONS:

1. It is recommended that the cavalry reconnaissance troop authorized by current T/O & E for the Infantry Division be replaced by an Armored Cavalry Troop of approximate strenght of 200, and organized in general along the lines of that shown in Tab B.

FOR: 116   AGAINST: 18

PRESENTED AT ROUND TABLE DISCUSSION:

Lt Col. R.E. Moore: Proposes that the words "armored cavalry troop" be deleted and substitute therefore "infantry reconnaissance company.".

FOR: 14

Appendix No. 2

**Intelligence and Reconnaissance Agencies —
Infantry Regiment**

O-5

THE INFANTRY CONFERENCE

FORT BENNING, GEORGIA

R E P O R T   O F   C O M M I T T E E

O N   O R G A N I C A T I O N

SHORT TITLE

INTELLIGENCE AND RECONNAISSANCE AGENCIES—INFANTRY REGIMENT

(O-5)

PRIORITY NUMBER

2

June 1946

ORGANIZATION OF THE COMMITTEE

Brigadier General Frederick McCabe — Chairman

Colonel William W. O'Connor, Infantry — Secretary

SUBCOMMITTEE PREPARING THE REPORT

Colonel Vennard Wilson, Cavalry — Chairman

Colonel Bernard A. Byrne, Infantry

Lieutenant Colonel Ellis W. Williamson, Infantry

Lieutenant Colonel Frank S. Holcombe, Infantry

Major Edward W. McGregor, Infantry

Major Hunter M. Montgomery, Infantry

OTHER COMMITTEE MEMBERS

Colonel R. W. Zwicker, GSC (Infantry)

Colonel M. J. Young, Engineer

Colonel John T. O'Neill, Engineer

Colonel R. J. Meyer, Signal

Colonel J. A. Dabney, Infantry

Lieutenant Colonel John Williamson, Infantry

Lieutenant Colonel E. D. Van Alstyne, Infantry

Lieutenant Colonel G. A. Nida, Ordnance

Lieutenant Colonel W. M. Summers, Infantry

Lieutenant Colonel D. A. King, Field Artillery

Lieutenant Colonel W. C. Chapman, Infantry

Lieutenant Colonel Carlyle F. McDannel, Infantry

Major Herbert F. Crecelius, Chemical Warfare Service

Major William R. Lynch, Jr., Infantry

Major George S. Beatty, Jr., Infantry

Major Lawson E. Hahn, Infantry

TABULATION OF COMMITTEE VOTE

RECOMMENDATIONS

	No. 1		No. 2		No. 3		No. 4		No. 5		No. 6		No.	
	Yes	No	Yes	No	Yes	No	Yes	No	Yes	No	Yes	No	Yes	No
Brig.Gen.F. McCabe	X		X		X		X		X		X			
Col. V. Wilson	X		X		X		X		X		X			
Col. B.A. Byrne	X		X		X		X		X		X			
Col. R.W. Zwicker	X		X		X		X		X		X			
Col. M. J. Young	Officer departed in compliance with orders prior to presentation of this study.													
Col. J. T. O'Neill	X		X		X		X		X		X			
Col. R. J. Meyor	X		X			X	X		X		X			
Col. J. A. Dabney	X		X		X		X		X		X			
Lt.Col.J.Williamson	X		X			X	X		X		X			
Lt.Col.E.D. Van Alstyne	X		X		X		X		X		X			
Lt.Col.E.W.Williamson	X		X		X		X		X		X			
Lt.Col.F.S. Holcombe	X		X			X	X		X		X			
Lt. Col. G. A. Nida	X		X		X		X		X		X			
Lt.Col.W. M. Summers	X		X			X	X		X		X			
Lt. Col. D. A. King	X		X		X		X		X		X			
Lt. Col. W. C. Chapman	X		X		X		X		X		X			
Lt. Col. C. F. McDaniel	X		X		X		X		X		X			
Major E. W. McGregor	X		X		X		X		X		X			
Major H. M. Montgomery	X		X		X		X		X		X			
Major H. F. Crecelius	Sitting and voting with Comm Tactics 'A' during this meeting.													
Major W. R. Lynch Jr.	X		X			X	X		X		X			
Major G. S. Beatty Jr.	X		X		X		X		X		X			
Major L. E. Hahn	X		X			X	X		X		X			
TOTALS	21		21		15	6	21		21		21			

THE INFANTRY CONFERENCE
FORT BENNING, GEORGIA

15 June 1946

SUBJECT: Intelligence and Reconnaissance Agencies, Infantry Regiment

    I. Papers accompanying

        1. Bibliography (Tab A)

        2. Testimonials (Tab B)

        3. Extracts (Tab C)

    II. The study presented

        Are the intelligence and reconnaissance agencies within the infantry regiment properly organized and equipped (to include battle patrols)? If not, in general, how should these agencies be organized and equipped?

    III. Facts bearing on the case

        1. Intelligence and reconnaissance agencies currently included within the infantry regiment and performing intelligence functions as their primary mission are found in the regimental and battalion headquarters companies as follows:

           a. Regimental intelligence and reconnaissance platoon (T/O & E 7-12). "The principal mission of the regimental intelligence and reconnaissance platoon is to serve as the special intelligence agency of the regimental commander for the collection of information under the supervision of the regimental intelligence officer (S-2). The platoon is also charged with counterintelligence measures and surveillance"(Par 9, FM 7-25).

           b. Battalion intelligence section(T/O & E 7-16) while not expressly defined, the mission of the section is apparent from the following statements concerning personnel who compose the section.

"Intelligence sergeant. In charge of battalion observation post(s) and intelligence observer scouts; operates at observation post or with patrols; may assist operations sergeant, especially in work for S-2" (Par 52c FM 7-20).

"Intelligence observer scouts. Operate observation post(s) or accompany front line units, patrols, raiding parties or reconnaissance and security detachments as intelligence scouts"(Par 52f FM 7-20).

2. Intelligence personnel are required to assist the intelligence officer in battalion and regimental command posts in the maintenance of maps and records, collation of intelligence and preparation and distribution of maps and sketches.

3. The preponderance of opinion obtained from battle experienced commanders indicates that the foregoing elements as now constituted are inadequate in personnel, grades, and ratings, automatic weapons, means of communication and specialized intelligence equipment.

4. A battle patrol unit is accepted as being one capable of employing its force as a unit or in part for combat patrolling to obtain intelligence or harrass the enemy or to perform security missions. Exceptionally, it may operate as a unit in offensive action.

5. Ten regiments are known to have organized and successfully employed battle patrol units composed of specially selected men. These units were usually composed of volunteers and given preferential treatment when not in action. Many commanders express the need for a battle unit within the infantry regiment.

6. On the other hand, a considerable number of commanders express the view that collection of qualified men in a battle patrol unit removes from the line companies the outstanding men around whom the combat efficiency of the company is built. They further feel that relief of these companies from battle patrolling lowers the overall performance of the command.

7. While proposals have been made that scout cars, light tanks and armored troop carriers be included in regimental I&R units, a substantial majority of the available opinions of experienced leaders favor the $\frac{1}{4}$-ton trucks as transport and regard armor as unsuitable for infantry reconnaissance units.

8. There is a widely expressed need for improved binocular telescopes, more compasses and more watches for regimental intelligence personnel.

IV. Conclusions.

1. There is need for increased strength, including appropriate grades, for the regimental I&R platoon and for an increase in automatic weapons and communication equipment within the platoon.

2. There is need for a regimental unit especially trained and equipped to perform battle patrols when efficient performance of such missions is beyond the capacity of line companies. These, however, should be special organizations created by the commander to meet his needs.

3. There is need in the infantry battalion headquarters for a small intelligence and reconnaissance unit capable of performing missions as now defined for the regimental I&R platoon.

4. Headquarters of both the infantry regiment and battalion require adequate assistants to the unit intelligence officer for CP operation of the S-2 section without diversion of personnel from intelligence, reconnaissance, and patrol duties.

5. There is need for an efficient binocular telescope for use of intelligence personnel. These personnel also require a liberal issue of compasses and watches.

6. Night vision equipment should be made available to intelligence units consistent with the suitability as proven by progressive development.

V. Recommendations, It is recommended that:

1. The regimental intelligence and reconnaissance platoon be increased to approximately one (1) officer and forty (40) men with three (3) squad organization and no change in currently assigned missions and that this platoon be provided with adequate communication and intelligence specialist equipment and high percentage of automatic weapons.

2. Intelligence sections of the regimental and battalion headquarters be provided with sufficient personnel to effectively assist the unit intelligence officer in operation of the S-2 section of the command post.

3. An intelligence and reconnaissance squad be included in the headquarters of each battalion trained and equipped to perform duties, including dismounted and motorized patrolling, as now prescribed for the regimental I & R platoon.

4. Adequate communication equipment be provided for the regimental I & R platoon to include one radio set as used in the regimental command net for the platoon headquarters and one for each squad.

5. An efficient binocular telescope be provided for use of intelligence personnel and these personnel liberally supplied with compasses and watches.

6. Infantry intelligence personnel be supplied with night vision equipment as proven appropriate by current development.

VI. Concurrences

The committee concurs in the foregoing conclusions and recommendations.

/s/ FREDERICK MC CABE

/t/ FREDERICK MC CABE
Brigadier General, U. S. A.
Chairman

BIBLIOGRAPHY

1. T/O & E 7-12 Headquarters & Headquarters Company, Infantry Regiment.

2. T/O & E 7-16 Headquarters & Headquarters Company, Infantry Battalion.

3. FM 7-20 Infantry Battalion.

4. FM 7-25 Headquarters Company, Intelligence and Signal Communications Rifle Regiment.

	Code No.	File No.	Date	Author
5. Preparation of Intelligence Field Manuals	G2,D.D.AGF	3 0274	30 Jun 45	E.O.Foster, Lt. Col.,AG of S,G2 Hq.91st Inf Div.
6. Report on Patrols	G2,D.D.AGF	3 0274	1 Mar 45	Sam Schlankey,Jr. Major, GSC Acting G2 Hq 91st Inf Div.
7. AGF Observers Board Report No.495 ETO	G2 - AGF	C 495	1 Jan 45	Albert G. Wing Colonel, Inf.
8. AGF Observers Board, G3 AFHQ ADV CP	G2 - AGF	A-147-1	16 Apr 44	
9. Battle Patrols	Ltr-TIS	Ltr-TIS		Ben Harrell Colonel, Inf.

TESTIMONIAL

Major General W. F. Dean, Assistant Division Commander and Division
Commander, 44th Infantry Division (ETO)

I have been told by officers in whom I have great confidence and
who were there, that a battle patrol for special patrol missions proved advantageous in several isolated instances, such as Anzio.

However, it is an organization that we cannot afford to carry in
our T/Os as a permanent unit. It is a luxury. It is my conviction
that the accomplishment of patrol missions should be part of every
well-trained infantryman's duties. In special circumstances, such as
at Anzio, it may be necessary to form a small provisional unit but they
should return to their parent organizations on termination of that
phase of the campaign.

In my limited combat experience I did not find that the requirement for an especially constituted battle patrol existed. My infantry
regiments were always capable of making all battle patrols and raids
desired. When on the defensive the battle patrols provided a means for
keeping alive an aggressive offensive spirit. When on the offensive
my battle patrols were well conducted by the units that would later
advance over that same terrain. I do not favor adding a special job
unit to perform a function which my infantry and attached Cav platoon
are competent to perform and which makes them better combat troops
for having done it.

Brigadier General E. S. Ott, Commanding General XV Corps Artillery (ETO)

1. Believe each rifle unit must be capable of performing successful combat patrol missions.

2. To accomplish above, rifle units need talent (bold, resource-
ful, energetic men) to lead the remainder.

3. Believe a special unit formed in the regiment would strip out this talent and thus lessen effectiveness of rifle units; and that it could not perform all the combat missions by itself.

4. Therefore, I believe in no special "prima donna" combat patrol unit.

Colonel J. H. Cochran, Infantry, Commanding Officer 415th Infantry, 104th Infantry Division (ETO)

1. I believe that the battle patrols for the regiment should come from the I&R platoon. Men in this platoon should be especially selected and trained for this purpose as well as for reconnaissance.

2. Battle patrols put out by a battalion should come from men in that battalion. If the training of this battalion has been good and men selected for patrol are of the right type, there will be no need for a special group in the regiment for battle patrol purposes.

3. I am opposed to forming a special group for this purpose since by so doing you are limiting the number of men in a rifle company.

Colonel J. F. R. Seitz, Infantry, Commanding Officer, 26th Infantry, 1st Infantry Division and Assistant Division Commander (ETO)

Reasons governing my decision that an especially constituted battle patrol within the infantry regiment is not desirable are as follows:

1. Such an organization would inevitably skim off the cream of the rifle companies, that is, leaders and potential leaders who have spirit and aggressiveness. This would be a continuing process for as losses occur in the patrol, replacements — the best — would have to come from the rifle companies.

2. If a special group is organized for patrolling, company

- 9 -

commanders will surely feel that it is then the job of higher headquarters to get information to the front. This is in violation of
basic military principle and intelligence and local security will
suffer materially.

3. Unless such a group is extremely and therefore uneconomical-
ly large, the number of operating patrols for a given twenty-four
hour period will be small. This is unsound for as this reduction
occurs one counter-intelligence screen is reduced and our local
intelligence gathering agencies are reduced. Experience has shown
that vigorous patrolling will keep the enemy "off our necks."

4. Specialists trend to become stereotyped. New patrol leaders
and members add variety to methods and solutions and help keep the
enemy off balance.

5. Patrols coming from companies that are to operate over areas
they are patrolling will be of more value to the company commander in
that he may use the patrol members as guides and not rely on a written
report.

6. I reiterate, I not only have no objection to, but do urge
that a slightly augmented I&R platoon do the distant patrolling -
patrols over 12 hours duration. These are few and require few men;
but the companies cannot relegate their patrolling to another agency
any more than the squad may relegate the duties of its scouts to some-
one else.

Colonel A. S. Newman, Infantry, Commanding Officer, 34th Infantry (SWPA)

Inclusion of an especially constituted battle patrol within the infantry regiment results in picking the best fighting man for these
special jobs. This takes away the spark plugs - and it is the few
spark plugs that make any unit go - and thus you have weakened the
units far more than by just taking a few men away.

2. Battle patrols -- which are nothing more or less than combined combat-intelligence patrols -- should be done by line units, without creating the idea that they should call on somebody else to do this tough job for them.

3. If it is desired to have one unit do this job, a line company can be given the job, and it should then be a rotated duty among all line companies.

Colonel W. J. Mullen, Infantry, Commanding Officer, 169th Infantry, 43d Infantry Division (Pacific)

Depending upon the mission any group of men, within a well trained infantry regiment, starting from one man and working on up through the squad, platoon, company, and battalion can handle any battle patrol.

To create a special so-called battle patrol merely takes men from the rifle companies.

A special battle patrol cannot accomplish all the battle patrolling necessary within a regiment; men need some rest and are not bulletproof.

Colonel T. M. Stark, Infantry, CofS, 25th Infantry Division (Pacific)

My decision, as recently expressed, that inclusion of an especially constituted battle patrol within the infantry regiment is not desirable, is based on my experience in the Luzon Campaign and my belief in keeping specially trained groups to a minimum in the basic arm as an organic part (keeping these efficiently trained after battle losses and attrition, etc.).

Colonel Douglas Sugg, Infantry, Commanding Officer, 27th Infantry, 25th Infantry Division (Pacific) and 345th Infantry (ETO)

Experience in the early part of World War II proved that the

employment of assault troops in the patrol mission to get information or for combat missions in or behind the enemy lines was
unsatisfactory. The need for expert performance of these missions led in my experience to the formation of volunteer "Tiger
Patrols" of one officer and 20 men each within each battalion.
These men lived in the battalion area, were acquainted at all
times with the situation and performed the assigned mission in a
superior manner.

Colonel E. F. Easterbrook, Infantry, Commanding Officer, 475th Infantry (CBI)

The mission of battle patrols requires specialization, men who
are adaptable to stealth, quick decision, determination, etc.

The average soldier cannot accomplish the mission, perhaps
because of lack of ability, perhaps because of over-extended ex-
ertion.

The importance of the mission is great and warrants specially-
qualified teams to execute the mission.

Lieutenant Colonel R. E. Moore, Infantry, Bn & Rogtl Commander, 3d
Infantry Division (ETO)

My decision, as recently expressed, that inclusion of an especially constituted battle patrol within the infantry regiment is
desirable, is based on the following reasons:
(1) All other means of performing difficult patrol missions proved
to be only partially successful. (2) The "battle patrol" as organized in my regiment never failed in a mission. (3) Casualties
in this trained battle patrol were low compared with those in in-
experienced patrols employed on similar missions, and (4) Means
must be found to reduce the heavy burden of patrolling from the
rifle company soldiers. He is not relieved of patrolling entirely.

and he should not so be, but he cannot fight every day and patrol
every night with success in both.

Colonel H. J. P. Harding, Infantry, AGF Observer, ETO, and Commanding Officer, 410th Infantry (ETO)

As an AGF Observer, I talked to officers and men of 3d Div
battle patrol at Anzio. Also, first combat action of my regiment
was to relieve 30th Inf, 3d Div, in France, and I saw something of
their use of a battle patrol.

I believe that the missions for which battle patrols were organized and used can, and should, be performed by the I&R platoon.
Have concurred with proposal to strengthen this platoon. Can see
no need for both a strengthened I&R platoon and special battle patrols. Doctrine of use of I&R platoon should not limit its employment so that two similar units would be necessary.

Colonel B. W. Brady, Infantry, Commanding Officer, 339th Infantry,
85th Div (Italy) and Executive Officer, 15th Infantry, 3d Division
(Italy)

My decision, as recently expressed, that inclusion of an especially constituted battle patrol within the infantry regiment is
desirable, is based on the following:

This proposal came up several times overseas. I wanted to try
it in my regiment but lack of training time out of the line prevent-
ed reorganization. Since many capable officers have expressed an
interest, I believe it should be given a trial.

Furthermore, it will greatly increase interest in the further
development of battle patrol technique in time of peace.

This proposal is based on the consideration that other regimental intelligence units remain small and perform "Reconnaissance

in force" only in exceptional circumstances.

Colonel P. H. Mahoney, Infantry, Commanding Officer, 20th Infantry,
(SWPA)

The regimental commander is frequently confronted in his operational area with civilian disorders, warring guerrilla factions,
terrorizing enemy parties and difficult long range contacts with
adjacent units. Delegation of these problems to battalions or
withdrawal of units from the battalions for these pressing missions
greatly distracts and impairs the main effort of the regiment. I
see a definite need for a "battle patrol" force immediately available to the regimental commander.

The Japanese Imperial Army was most adept in infiltration
tactics. Sensitive and vulnerable rear installations were always
in great danger. Immediate response to reported enemy movements
was mandatory. The battle patrol provides the answer. Of course
there is always local security established but the battle patrol
would be the striking force.

I do not condone giving the battle patrol a sustained load of
extremely hazardous duty. This only decimates the patrol and de-
stroys morale. This patrol is easily abused. If a difficult contact indicates a reinforced company then a battle patrol should
not be used.

This aggressive unit can insure a regimental operation from
dislocation by enemy infiltration parties.

Colonel W. W. O'Connor, Infantry, C of S, 76th Infantry Division
(ETO)

My decision, as recently expressed, that inclusion of an especially constituted battle patrol within the infantry regiment
is desirable, is based on the following:

Experiences of divisions that were in protracted combat indicated that the personnel needed for execution of the more difficult patrol missions were too whipped to accomplish it. Rest and special consideration for this personnel were necessary.

Centralization and special training inherent in the proposed system would indicate a greater number of successful missions. Perhaps rotation, rest, and recuperation is the answer to this. Apparently units in the Pacific, where operation periods were of shorter duration, had little trouble in getting effective results by using methods prescribed in our manuals.

EXTRACTS

1. Recommendations of CG 91st Inf. Div.:

   a. Recommend Regimental I & R Platoon be increased to strength of 36 men to allow for increased S-2 personnel and increased patrolling by the platoon.

   b. Recommend Infantry Battalion intelligence sections be increased 12 men for increased patrolling and intelligence functioning.

2. Report of AGF Observer in ETO (Col. A.G. Wing, Inf.):

   1. Col. Sterling Wood, CO 313th Inf, 79th Inf, Div.:

   Every ¼ ton in the I & R platoon should be equipped with this weapon (50 cal MG HB) as standard equipment. We have equipped ours in this manner and find that they can really go places and perform missions that would be impossible without this armament.

3. Report by Lt. Col. Brennan, Inf. Bn. Comdr., on Intelligence Section, Infantry Battalion:

   a. Organization

   Personnel should be increased to 10 or 12 men in this section. This is necessary to provide adequate men to man two Bn. OPs 24 hours a day and to have sufficient intelligence personnel at the battalion CP to handle interrogation of PWs, maps and other S-2 functions. Casualty rates also necessitate increased personnel. Col. Powers' battalion had about 200% replacement in his intelligence section in an 8 month period. I had a 75% replacement over a similar period.

   b. Ratings

   The lowest rating in the section should be a T/5. Each man in the section is a specialist and recognition should be given him for his ability. We picked our replacements from rifle companies; men who were mature, intelligent

   - that'

and "battle wise." In most cases these men have served in the intelligence section as a private whereas had they remained in a rifle company they would have been a squad leader in a very short time.

4. Report of Lt. Col. M. J. Peale Jr. CO 3d Bn, 161st Inf:

. The R Bn should have a Rcn plat that can operate both on foot and on vehicles. A Lt Tk Rcn Co in the Inf Regt could do the job so that there would be a plat for each Bn CO and one for the Regtl CO. The Tk should be light to cross small wooden bridges and should be capable of moving over muddy ground as the M-8 is not. An organization like that of the platoons of the Div Rcn troops would do the job.

5. Maj. Gen. O'Daniel, CG 3d Inf Div (10 Apr 44):

As a result of operations on this beachhead, I have become convinced that we must have the equivalent of the World War I scout platoon to carry out the deep patrols and raids where skilled, determined men are essential to success. We are now organizing such a Battle Patrol group in the division and also in each infantry regiment. All members of these patrols are volunteers who want to get into close combat with the German.

6. Scouting and Patrolling, AGF Board Report by Col. G. E. Parker. (Extract)

* * * * *

5. Augmentation of Battalion Intelligence Sections. In five of the six divisions it was customary to augment battalion intelligence sections. These sections, as constituted in current T/O and E were considered barely adequate for office work and manning OPs and augmentations were generally for patrolling.

* * * * *

69th Division: Enlisted men in the battalion intelligence platoon should be hand picked and their ratings should be high, mostly sergeant and above. Tables should include transportation for the whole platoon, radios, and a high proportion of automatic weapons so that patrols can handle sudden situations and can fight for their information when they have to.

7. Report of Lt. Col. M. O. Edwards, GSC, AGF Observer, ETO (Extract).

Each infantry battalion headquarters company needs a reconnaissance platoon of 30 men, specially trained for reconnaissance patrols. These men would relieve rifle companies of this work (though not of security, contact patrols, etc).

8. Report of Col. A. G. Wing, Inf. WD Observer, ETO. (Extract)

Battle Patrols. Two regiments of the 3rd Infantry Division, 7th Inf and 30th Inf use battle patrols, Lt. Col. John A. Heintges, CO 7th Inf, 3rd Inf Div:

"Our battle patrol is based on the I & R Platoon of the regimental headquarters company, reinforced to strength of 3 officers and 45 enlisted men. This patrol has 11 ¼ ton trucks, armored to protect personnel against shell fragments, and armed with .30 cal and .50 cal machine guns. The patrol is divided into three (3) sections which are used as a base of fire section, an assault section, and a reconnaissance section. Sections are interchangeable for these purposes. * * * * The men of the battle patrol are picked men.* * * * They are strongly armed with automatic weapons, preferring the sub machine gun for a personal weapon."

9. Comments of Gen. Hibbs, Comdt. FAS.

The I & R platoon is too small to perform its assigned mission. It is suggested that it be organized similarly to a platoon of the division reconnaissance troop and that light tanks be provided in lieu of the scout car.

THE INFANTRY CONFERENCE
FORT BENNING, GEORGIA

20 June 1946

APPENDIX 1.

<u>CONFERENCE DISCUSSION</u>

COMMITTEE REPORT PRESENTED

    O-5 Are the intelligence and reconnaissance agencies
within the infantry regiment properly organized and equipped
(to include battle patrols)? If not, in general how should
these agencies be organized and equipped?

DISCUSSION

    None.

THE INFANTRY CONFERENCE
FORT BENNING, GEORGIA

21 June 1946

COMPILATION OF CONFERENCE VOTE

QUESTION: O-5

Are the intelligence and reconnaissance agencies within the infantry regiment properly organized and equipped (to include battle patrols?) If not, in general, how should these agencies be organized and equipped?

RECOMMENDATIONS:

1. The regimental intelligence and reconnaissance platoon be increased to approximately one (1) officer and forty (40) men with three (3) squad organization and no change in currently assigned missions and that this platoon be provided with adequate communication and intelligence specialist equipment and high percentage or automatic weapons.

   FOR: 112   AGAINST: 3

2. Intelligence sections of the regimental and battalion headquarters be provided with sufficient personnel to effectively assist the unit intelligence officer in operation of the S-2 section of the command post.

   FOR: 118   AGAINST: 1

3. An intelligence and reconnaissance squad be included in the headquarters of each battalion trained and equipped to perform duties, including dismounted and motorized patrolling, as now prescribed for the regimental I & R Platoon.

   FOR: 108   AGAINST: 10

4. Adequate communication equipment be provided for the regimental I & R platoon to include one radio set as used in the regimental command net for the platoon headquarters and one for each squad.

   FOR: 120   AGAINST: 0

5. An efficient binocular telescope be provided for use of intelligence personnel and these personnel liberally supplied with compasses and watches.

   FOR: 120   AGAINST: 1

6. Infantry intelligence personnel be supplied with night vision equipment as proven appropriate by current development.

   FOR: 121   AGAINST: 0

APPENDIX NO 2

WRITTEN COMMENTS:

Lt Col A. M. Murray: Propose that committee recommendation 5 be reworded to include the following pharse; "that improved observation instruments -------". This phrase to replace; "in place of binocular scopes".

Lt Col W. M. Summers: (Ref. committee recommendation 3) There is no need for such a unit in the infantry battalion, but additional personnel for efficient operation on a 24 hours basis, of one (1) or more battalion OP's, be provided in the battalion intelligence section.

Defense Platoon—Division Headquarters
O-6

THE INFANTRY CONFERENCE

FORT BENNING, GEORGIA

R E P O R T   O F   C O M M I T T E E

O N   O R G A N I Z A T I O N

SHORT TITLE
DEFENSE PLATOON
DIVISION HEADQUARTERS

(0-6)

PRIORITY NUMBER

(14)

June 46

ORGANIZATION OF THE COMMITTEE

Brigadier General Frederick McCabe	Chairman
Colonel William W. O'Connor, Infantry	Secretary
Major John McWatters, Infantry	Asst. Secretary

SUB-COMMITTEE PREPARING THE REPORT

Colonel J. A. Dabney, Infantry	Chairman
Lieutenant Colonel W. C. Chapman, Infantry	Member
Lieutenant Colonel Carlyle F. McDannel, Infantry	Member
Major George S. Beatty Jr., Infantry	Member

OTHER COMMITTEE MEMBERS

Colonel R. W. Zwicker, GSC (Infantry)

Colonel M. J. Young, Engineers

Colonel J. T. O'Neill, Engineers

Colonel R. J. Meyer, Signal

Colonel Vennard Wilson, Cavalry

Colonel B. A. Byrne, Infantry

Lieutenant Colonel Frank S. Holcombe, Infantry

Lieutenant Colonel D. A. King, Field Artillery

Lieutenant Colonel G. A. Nida, Ordnance

Lieutenant Colonel W. M. Summers, Infantry

Lieutenant Colonel John Williamson, Infantry

Lieutenant Colonel Ellis W. Williamson, Infantry

Lieutenant Colonel E. D. Van Alstyne, Infantry

Major Herbert F. Crecelius, Chemical Warfare Service

Major Lawson E. Hahn, Infantry

Major William R. Lynch Jr., Infantry

Major Edward E. McGregor, Infantry

Major Hunter M. Montgomery, Infantry

- 1 -

TABULATION OF COMMITTEE VOTE

RECOMMENDATIONS

	No. 1		No. 2		No.		No.		No.		No.	
	Yes	No	Yes	No	Yes	No	Yes	No	Yes	No	Yes	No
Brig. Gen. F. McCabe	X		X									
Col. V. Wilson	X		X									
Col. B. A. Byrne	X		X									
Col. R. W. Zwicker	X		X									
Col. M. J. Young	Officer departed in compliance with orders before presentation of this study.											
Col. J. T. O'Neill	X		X									
Col. R. J. Meyer	X		X									
Col. J. A. Dabney	X		X									
Lt. Col. J. Williamson	X		X									
Lt. Col. E. D. Van Alstyne	X		X									
Lt. Col. E. W. Williamson	X		X									
Lt. Col. F. S. Holcombe	X		X									
Lt. Col. G. A. Nida	X		X									
Lt. Col. W. M. Summers	X		X									
Lt. Col. D. A. King	X		X									
Lt. Col. W. C. Chapman	X		X									
Lt. Col. C. F. McDannel	X		X									
Major E. W. McGregor	X		X									
Major H. M. Montgomery	X		X									
Major H. F. Crecelius	Officer sitting and voting with Com. Tactics "A" during presentation of this study.											
Major W. R. Lynch Jr.	X		X									
Major G. S. Beatty Jr.	X		X									
Major L. E. Hahn	X		X									

TOTALS   21   21

SUBJECT: Defense Platoon - Infantry Division

I. Papers accompanying

1. Bibliography (Tab A)

2. Testimonials (Tab B)

3. Extracts from Statements (Tab C)

II, The Study Presented

Should the defense platoon of division headquarters be retained? If so, in general how should this platoon be organized and equipped?

III. Facts Bearing on the Study

a. The key installation of an Infantry Division is the Division CP, and to assure success of the division in combat, the CP must remain operational twenty-four (24) hours a day.

b. To assure continous operation of the Division Cp in Combat, adequate protection must be provided at all times.

c. The Division CP may be subjected to attacks from ground forces, including tanks, airborne troops and aircraft.

d. The defense platoon as presently organized is equipped to provide anti-mechanized protection but is short of riflemen. T/O. & E 7-2, 1 June 1945, authorizes one (1) officer and twenty-nine (29) enlisted men armed with three (3) 57 MM recoulless rifles, three (3) 50 caliber HB MG, six (6) 2.36 rocket launchers, six (6) 45 caliber pistols, five (5) M1 rifles and nineteen (19) 30 caliber carbines.

e. Combat experiences of fourteen (14) divisions of both the Pacific and European Theaters show a definite need of more infantry type personnel within the defense platoon, to provide protection against infiltrating ground troops.

f. The general board U.S. Forces European Theater made the following statement:

"The personnel at present assigned to headquarters
company is adequate for efficient operation of the division
command post. During the European Campaign some divisions
augmented this company, but there is no evidence that additional
personnel is needed permanently."

g. However, to provide adequate defense of the Division CP,
many units found it to be necessary to augment the defense platoon
with personnel from other organic elements of the division, princi-
pally the division band, MP platoon, Rcn Troop and rifle platoons
from rifle companies. This defensive mission is not the primary
function of these units. The robbing of rifle companies of personnel
to defend the division command post is particularly objectionable.

IV. Conclusions

1. The defense platoon should be retained in Division
Headquarters to provide the Division CP with adequate protection
in order to assure continous operation in combat.

2. The defense platoon as presently organized lacks
sufficient rifle strength to provide an effective perimeter defense
and to provide the interior guard of the Division CP.

3. A rifle platoon is a desirable organization to
provide the necessary rifle strength. This rifle strength should be
augmented with an antimechanized defense. A motorized section of
approximately eleven enlisted men would be capable of manning three
(3) 75 MM recoulless rifles. The rifle se:tion should be given six
(6) rocket launchers as extra equipment.

4. A rifle platoon reinforced with a small but effective
antimechanized section is the best organization to defend the Division
CP.

V. Recommendations

1. The defense platoon be retained as an organic element
of Division Headquarters Company.

2. That a sufficient increase of personnel be authorized to provide a platoon headquarters, a rifle section, and a weapons section. The total strength of the platoon to be approximately one (1) officer and fifty-two (52) enlisted men armed and equipped to perform the primary mission of the unit.

VI. Concurrences.

The committee concurs in the foregoing conclusions and recommendations.

/s/
Frederick McCabe
Brigadier General, U S A
Chairman

ORGANIZATION NO. 4

<u>TESTIMONIAL</u>

Lt. Colonel Herman H. Kesser, Infantry.

Based upon my experience as headquarters commandant, G-3, 87th Division, 2 mos; G-3, 85th Division, 11 mos.

Q. Should the defense platoon of a division headquarters be retained?

A. Yes, in augmented form.

Q. Is the strength of a platoon as we now have -- 29 enlisted men and one officer -- sufficient to perform the primary missions?

A. No. They are neither of sufficient size nor of proper composition.

Q. What increase in strength would you recommend?

A. The main increase should be in the rifle element of approximately three (3) squads.

Q. Would you recommend that the platoon be organized into two (2) sections -- antitank and rifle?

A. Yes.

Q. Should pioneer personnel be incorporated into the platoon in any element?

A. No.

Q. Should the platoon be authorized any additional equipment other than that now in TO&E ?

A. None, other than equipment for the additional rifles -- no special equipment.

Q. Is the rank of first lieutenant commensurate with this command?

A. Yes, I think so because the primary responsibility belongs to the headquarters commandant.

Q. What do you think the primary mission of a defense platoon should be?

A. A close-in perimeter defense against infiltrating ground forces to include armor.

Q. Do you consider interior guard duty to be a part of a primary mission?

A. Yes. I consider it to be a full time primary job to defent the CP and this mission cannot be adequately accomplished by other troops organic to the CP setup who have other primary missions.

Lt. Colonel Herman Hicks, Jr., Infantry.

Based upon my experience as Regimental S-4, 13 mos; Battalion Commander, 17 mos; Headquarters Commandant, 10 mos.

I concur in the remarks made by Lt. Colonel Kessler with the exception that I recommend some study be made to determine the size of this organization. It is felt that it could become too un-wieldly; therefore, I feel that some study should be made to limit this to a platoon of 48 to 56 men — total anti-tank section and rifle section included— to be commanded by one officer in the grade of first lieutenant, assisted by a technical sergeant as section chief of each section.

Bibliography

Title

	Code No.	File No.	Date	Author
1. Hq. Co., Inf Div. T/O & E 7-2			1 June 45	W.D.
2. Inf. Rifle Co. T/O & E 7-17			1 June 45	W.D.
3. AGF Report Tactics & T/O Infantry Divisions	1088		14 Jul 45	W.D. Observers' Board Col. G. E. Parker

S E C R E T

HEADQUARTERS ARMY GROUND FORCES

1   29 September 1944

SUBJECT: Observer Report, European Theatre of Operation, 13 August –
20 September 1944.

C-3

1. b. The defense platoon was also considered inadequate and was sup-
plemental. In effect this platoon now consists of one rifle platoon, one
anti-tank platoon and four engineers who are used to check areas for mines
and booby-traps. This augmentation has been justified by an action which
took place on the morning of 8 September when a German Panzer brigade
slipped behind the combat elements of the division and struck the command
post at about 0200. The defense platoon gave an excellent account of itself in this action and amid the confusion forced the enemy to withdraw
to a defiladed position, permitting the movement of the command post to
another location. When the battle was resumed at daybreak the division
repelled the enemy, forcing him to attempt a withdrawal through our own
lines which failed utterly. The result of the action showed 30 enemy
tanks and 54 half-tracks destroyed and 750 prisoners taken.

                                        /s/ Donald L. Durfee
                                        DONALD L. DURFEE
                                        Lt. Col., Infantry

                                                    SECRET

2 A   HEADQUARTERS FOURTH ARMY
                             Fort Sam Houston, Texas

                                        6 June 1946

1. Necessary changes in Table of Organization of the Infantry, Airborne and Mountain Divisions.

    a. Should the defense platoon of division headquarters be re-
tained? Defense platoon of division headquarters should be retained.
This platoon furnished a close perimeter defense for the Div. C. P.

If this defense platoon is not an organic part of this headquarters, itt must be provided for by some lower unit which decreases the combat strength and efficiency of the unit and lessens its effectiveness in its primary duties.

In combat it should be considered a reward for especially meritorious service during long periods of combat.

COMMENTS GENERAL HIBBS
COMD FA SCHOOL
28 May 1946

Headquarters Company as at present organized is weak in personnel necessary to perform its mission in combat. I refer specifically to the units, the division defense platoon which will be discussed later and the special platoon. The special platoon in order to feed and otherwise service the division headquarters should be twice its present size. The transportation assigned by the T/O & E to division headquarters company transportation platoon is inadequate. Specifically, twenty-six jeeps are not enough to meet the requirements of combat with regard to the transportation of staff officers. This so-called economy in transportation is in fact uneconomical in maintainance, in driver fatigue with the accompanying accidents, and in the expeditious accomplishment of staff missions. No unit of divisional size can run a staff motor pool in combat; 40 jeeps are needed.

The defense platoon of division headquarters should be retained and should in fact be enlarged to twice its present strength. The personnel of this unit, shortly after a division enters combat should be used to replace casualities in the infantry regiments. Older men, or men who have been found unable to stand up under the stringencies of combat in the infantry regiment, should then be used to replace the personnel of the division defense platoon.

The grade of major is adequate for the division provost marshal. In this connection another possibility in the formation of a division defense platoon is to enlarge the military police company by fifty or sixty men and then rotate platoons used in defense of the division CP.

- 10 -

File 320.2/9   Study No 15 (F15)

Par 1c (1) Headquarters Company

The personnel at present assigned to headquarters company is adequate for efficient operation of the division command post. During the European Campaign some divisions augmented this company but there is not evidence that additional personnel is needed permanently.

4

Annex A
Combat Experiences

1. European Theater:

   30th Div - Augmented defense platoon with band; was not satisfactory.

   69th Div - Used Div Ren Trp or tank reconnaissance personnel.

   76th Div - Organic platoon never adequate. Got security platoon from regiment. At times used Ren Trp.

   78th Div - Augmented with 50 cal AAA, Band, and at times Ren Trp.

   87th Div - The Def Plat had two M-1 scout cars to use as escort guard for CG and Asst CG but they were never needed throughout the combat period. When considered necessary for CP defense, the Defense Plat was strengthened by one platoon from the Ren Troop. The AT gun was discarded for Inf type weapons since the AT guns were never fired in action.

   102 Div - Augmented defense platoon - method not indicated.

2. Mediterranean Theater (Italy):

   85th Div - Used elements of band, MP Plat, and Ren trp at various times. In breakthrough in Po Valley used rifle platoon from reserve Regt.

   88th Div - Reinforced by personnel from MP Plat which in turn was augmented by Div Band. The Plat was used as Inf. for perimeter Def. anti-mechanized elements never used or needed.

3. Pacific Theater:

The American Div - Used the T/O Plat on Bougainville but was never needed because of tight defense areas around Div CP by other units. However, on Philippine Islands, the Div CP was constantly harassed by Japs at night. Def. Plat. used as infantry and usually killed 10 to 12 Japs each night. Anti-mechanized elements not needed - only Inf type defense.

25th Div - Augmented by Div MP Co who were armed with tommy guns while on Guadalcanal. This force was still very unsatisfactory as Japs infiltrated the Div CP area and the MPs were fired on by other Americans because their tommy guns sounded like Jap guns. After this, all tommy guns were taken out of the Div as they were to inaccurate for this type of work and sounded too much like Japanese weapons. The Div CP needed infantrymen with Inf. Weapons.

5. Discussion by 37th Div on their Defense Platoon.

c. Defense. In many places the Defense Platoon was not of sufficient size adequately to man the perimeter defense. Prior to proceeding on this last operation, the personnel of the Division Band were trained in the use of automatic weapons and other phases of defense. Members of the various sections of headquarters were likewise trained. This porvided adequate personnel for the perimeter defense and only once during the six months of combat was it thought advisable to call upon any of the regiments for this purpose.

APPENDIX NO. 1   21 June 1946

CONFERENCE DISCUSSION

COMMITTEE REPORT PRESENTED

Q-6 Should the defense platoon of division headquarters be retained? If so, in general how should this
platoon be organized and equipped?

DISCUSSION

Lt. Col. Murray, WD G-4:

This defense platoon, as is outlined in these recommendations, is an integral part of the division headquarters
company which means it is composed generally of men who are
not combat experienced and, as such, in a great many experiences they were not satisfactory as a defense of the CP.
I recommend that a rifle platoon be drawn from combat units
for temporary assignment to division for these defense purposes. This platoon would be preferably a platoon that had
seen intense combat and could stand a little bit less arduous
work and could be depended upon to fight properly if the need
arose.

Brigadier General McCabe:

Do I understand your recommendation is that we take a
rifle platoon away from some organization and place it in the
defending division headquarters?

Lt. Col. Murray:

Yes, sir, that has been the opinion of a number of headquarters commandants with whom I have discussed this problem
in the past.

Major General J. W. O'Daniel, TIS:

It might have been the opinion of the headquarters
commandants but is not the opinion of the division commander.
No division commander I think, or headquarters, would desire
to rotate in the defending platoon experienced combat men and
build this same platoon up with those men. We did that in the
units I happened to be with and certainly I think that we are
violating something we have been holding out for here - that
is, not to cause attrition in rifle companies by administration.

THE INFANTRY CONFERENCE
FORT BENNING, GEORGIA

21 June 1946

COMPILATION OF CONFERENCE VOTE

QUESTION: C-6 "Should the defense platoon of division
  headquarters be retained? If so, in general how should
  this platoon be organized and equipped?

RECOMMENDATIONS:

1. The defense platoon be retained as an organic
    element of Division Headquarters Company.

FOR 117   AGAINST   5

2. That a sufficient increase of personnel be authorized
    to provide a platoon headquarters, a rifle section,
    and a weapons section. The total strength of the
    platoon to be approximately one (1) officer and
    fifty-two (52) enlisted men armed and equipped to
    perform the primary mission of the unit.

FOR 109   AGAINST 13

PRESENTED AT ROUND TABLE DISCUSSION:

Lt Col A. M. MURRAY: Reference committee
recommendation 2. Propose that rifle personnel
be drawn from combat units on a rational basis.

FOR: 2

WRITTEN COMMENTS:

Maj. Gen. W. F. DEAN: Reference committee
recommendation 2. Recommend that present
authorized strength be retained.

APPENDIX NO. 2

THE INFANTRY CONFERENCE

FORT BENNING, GEORGIA

R E P O R T   O F   C O M M I T T E E

O N   O R G A N I Z A T I O N

SHORT TITLE

SECURITY ELEMENT - REGIMENTAL HEADQUARTERS

(O-7)

PRIORITY NUMBER

(1)

June 1946

ORGANIZATION OF THE COMMITTEE

Brigadier General Frederick McCabe   Chairman

Colonel William W. O'Connor, Infantry   Secretary

SUBCOMMITTEE PREPARING THE REPORT

Lieutenant Colonel John Williamson, Infantry   Chairman

Lieutenant Colonel E. D. Van Alstyne, Infantry

OTHER COMMITTEE MEMBERS

Colonel R. W. Zwicker, GSC (Infantry)

Colonel M. J. Young, Engineer

Colonel John T. O'Neill, Engineer

Colonel R. J. Meyer, Signal

Colonel J. A. Dabney, Infantry

Colonel Vennard Wilson, Cavalry

Colonel Bernard A. Byrne, Infantry

Lieutenant Colonel G. A. Nida, Ordnance

Lieutenant Colonel W. M. Summers, Infantry

Lieutenant Colonel D. A. King, Field Artillery

Lieutenant Colonel W. C. Chapman, Infantry

Lieutenant Colonel Carlyle F. McDannel, Infantry

Lieutenant Colonel Ellis W. Williamson, Infantry

Lieutenant Colonel Frank S. Holcombe, Infantry

Major William R. Lynch, Jr., Infantry

Major George S. Beatty, Jr., Infantry

Major Lawson E. Hahn, Infantry

Major Edward W. McGregor, Infantry

Major Hunter M. Montgomery, Infantry

TABULATION OF COMMITTEE VOTE

RECOMMENDATIONS

	No. 1		No. 2	
	Yes	No	Yes	No
Brig. Gen. F. Mc Cabe	x		x	
Col. V. Wilson	x		x	
Col. B. A. Byrne	x		x	
Col. R. W. Zwicker	x		x	
Col. M. J. Young	x		x	
Col. J. T. O'Neill	x		x	
Col. R. C. Meyer	x		x	
Col. J. A. Dabney	x		x	
Lt. Col. J. Williamson	x		x	
Lt. Col. E. D. Van Alstyne	x		x	
Lt. Col. E. W. Williamson	x		x	
Lt. Col. F. S. Holcombe	x		x	
Lt. Col. G. A. Nida	x		x	
Lt. Col. W. M. Summers	x		x	
Lt. Col. D. A. King	x		x	
Lt. Col. W. C. Chapman	x		x	
Lt. Col. C. F. Mc Dannel	x		x	
Major E. W. McGregor	x		x	
Major H. M. Montgomery	x		x	
Major H. F. Crecelius Sitting and voting with committee - Tactics "A" during this meeting				
Major W. R. Lynch Jr.	x		x	
Major G. S. Beatty Jr.	x		x	
Major L. E. Hahn	x		x	
TOTALS	22		22	

THE INFANTRY CONFERENCE

FORT BENNING, GEORGIA

SUBJECT: Security Element -- Infantry Regiment

    I. Papers accompanying

        1. List of charts (Tab A)

        2. Testimonials (Tab B)

        3. Minority Report (Tab C)

    II. The study presented

        Is a security element necessary for regimental headquarters? If so, in general how should this unit be organized and equipped?

    III. Facts bearing on study

        The facts bearing on this study are the same as those discussed in question O-2 (M. P. Platoon). They are not to be discussed here.

    IV. Conclusions

        1. There is a need for an organic unit in the infantry regimental headquarters for military police duties.

        2. Such a unit should also provide security for the regimental C.P. in combat.

        3. The newly authorized division M.P. company cannot fulfill this need.

        4. A regimental band, if authorized, should not be used for these duties.

    V. Recommendations

        1. That a command post security and military police platoon be included as an organic element of the infantry regimental headquarters.

        2. That this platoon have a strength of about one officer and thirty-four enlisted men, with sufficient weapons and transportation to enable it to perform its duties. (See Chart in Tab A for suggested T/O & E)

VI. Concurrences

        The committee concurs in the foregoing conclusion and recommendations (except for minority report as attached).

/s/
FREDERICK McCABE
Brigadier General, U.S.A.
Chairman

4

The chart below shows a suggested organization for regimental military police and security platoon to be added to the Regimental Headquarters Company, T/O & E 7-12.

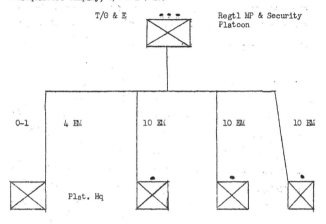

T/O & E   Regtl MP & Security Platoon

O-1   4 EM   10 EM   10 EM   10 EM

Plat. Hq

1-1st Lt Plat Comdr (CBN)

1-T/Sgt Plat   (CBN)

3-T/5 Drivers, truck (R)

EACH SQUAD

1-S/Sgt Squad Ldr (R)

1-Sgt Asst "   (R)

8-Pvts or PFC Rifleman (R)

2-Carbines Cal. .30

3-Rifles Cal. .30 M1

3-Launcher Grenade M7

1-MG HB Cal. .50

2-Trucks $\frac{1}{4}$-t

2-Trailers $\frac{1}{4}$-t

1-Truck $2\frac{1}{2}$-t

10-Rifle, Cal. .30 M1

3 Launcher Grenade M7

1 Launcher Rocket

TAB A

5

TESTIMONIAL

Major General William F. Dean, CG 44th Div.

I feel that it is necessary to have a small regimental
M.P. Unit (about 1 officer and 20 EM). My experience was that each
regimental commander organized one, even though at first I did not
feel that it was necessary. I found, however, that such an organization for M.P. duty and C.P. security was needed.

Lt. Col. John Williamson, Infantry

Based upon my experience as regimental executive,
Battalion Commander, and regimental commander in the 18th Infantry,
1st Infantry Division from 1942 to 1945, I believe a security and
military police platoon in regimental headquarters to be absolutely
essential. We used the regimental band for this purpose in Tunisia
and Sicily, but this was not satisfactory because the band had no
opportunity for practice for months and it could not play for several days after we got out of the front lines. When the band was
taken away from the regiments, we formed a so-called MP platoon of
an officer and 30 men. This platoon proved to be indispensible in
handling POWs, taking them from battalions, handling them at regiment, and when necessary, escorting them to the Division cage. It
was also used as guides for road marches and for command post security.

Col. Stanley R. Larsen, Infantry

Based on my experience as Commanding Officer of the 35th Infantry, 25th Inf Div, May 1944 to December 1945, I believe that a
security element is necessary for regimental headquarters.

If, under the present organization, all personnel are used
properly, there is insufficient means for a regimental headquarters
to be defended against infiltration and small raiding parties. In
the Pacific campaigns, it was always necessary to improvise a

TAB B

bastard defense unit for local perimeter protection at night, and
it was a daily worry for the Regimental Hq Co CO to revamp his local
security arrangement because from day to day the number of men he
had to work with changed. Practically all enlisted men had to pull
security duty at night. - For short periods this would be acceptable
to any soldier but over extended periods, and for those men, such as
radio operators, wiremen, cooks, runners, mechanics, drivers, etc.,
it is an excessive drain on one's physical and mental reserves to
have to spend half of each night on guard.

Whenever possible, we used our I & R platoon for local security
but, as often as not, they were out on O.P. duty. On Luzon we had
to rely on the questionable capabilities of self-styled guerillas to
keep our Regimental perimeter safe at night.

At no time during the war did I ever feel that our security was
adequate, and I have often wondered if this serious oversight (that
of providing proper Regtl Hq Security) would ever be corrected in
the T/O for the Inf Regt. - Naturally, there are many other more
serious omissions and deficiencies which should be corrected, too,
but this one cannot be overlooked.

My recommendation is that a reinforced platoon (about 60 men)
would be sufficiently strong enough to act as Regtl Hq Security.
It should be equipped with BAR's or other light automatic weapons,
and M-1's. The automatic rifles should be in the ratio of 1 to 6
or 7 rifles because most of the firing by security elements is
done at night and at close ranges, needing wide dispersion to cover
the target which cannot be clearly seen.

The platoon should be equipped with a 60mm mortar, mainly to
be used for firing flares at night. Sniper scopes should be issued
to the platoon (1 to every 8 men) sufficient to allow overlap in
coverage by them.

This platoon could serve as the Regimental MP platoon, functioning as such during the day when necessary or continuously in rear
and rest areas. Soldiers who have served well at the front and

deserve "light" duty for a change could keep this platoon filled
with battle season and well respected men.

Just as so many other things are overlooked and quickly forgotten in peace which, in war, were critically needed, so will
this little item of Regimental Security be minimized and soon
shelved, but in the next war our flexible T/O's will again be
called on to permit us to reestablish our make-shift means of
getting good security and having an MP establishment which
logically can be a part of the Regtl T/O.

THE INFANTRY CONFERENCE
THE INFANTRY SCHOOL
FORT BENNING, GEORGIA

15 June 1946

MEMORANDUM for Chairman, Committee on Organization.

SUBJECT: Minority Report No. 1.

The undersigned submits a minority report as follows:

1. Recommend that a band be a component part of any MP-Security unit that may be provided for the infantry regiment.

It is felt that:

a. A band is desirable for morale purposes.

b. A band whose sole mission is to play music, and which cannot have minor exposure to casualty is a luxury the unit cannot afford.

c. Immunity from danger and constant opportunity for practice is not essential to the quality of a band that can furnish entertainment as a primary mission and render ceremonial music as a secondary mission during combat.

2. In conclusion, it is contended that soldiers prefer dance music to formal band music and that an available "pick-up" orchestra, even though not highly proficient, is preferable to the occasional appearance of a formal band.

/s/ Bernard A. Byrne
BERNARD A. BYRNE
Colonel, Infantry

Tab C.

9

THE INFANTRY CONFERENCE
FORT BENNING, GEORGIA

19 June 1946

APPENDIX 1.

CONFERENCE DISCUSSION

COMMITTEE REPORT PRESENTED

O-7 Is a security element necessary for regimental headquarters?
If so, in general how should this unit be organized and equipped?

DISCUSSION

None.

THE INFANTRY CONFERENCE
FORT BENNING, GEORGIA

21 June 1946

COMPILATION OF CONFERENCE VOTE

QUESTION: O-7 "Is a security element necessary for regimental headquarters? If so, in general how should this unit be organized and equipped?

RECOMMENDATIONS:

1. That a command post security and military police platoon be included as an organic element of the infantry regimental headquarters.

FOR	AGAINST
120	4

2. That this platoon have a strength of about one officer and thirty-four enlisted men, with sufficient weapons and transportation to enable it to perform its duties. (See Chart in Tab 4 for suggested T/O & E)

MINORITY REPORT

1. Recommend that a band be a component part of any MP-Security unit that may be provided for the infantry regiment.

It is felt that:

FOR	AGAINST
117	7

a. A band is desirable for morale purposes.

b. A band whose sole mission is to play music, and which cannot have minor exposure to casualty is a luxury the unit cannot afford.

c. Immunity from danger and constant opportunity for practice is not essential to the quality of a band that can furnish entertainment as a primary mission and render ceremonial music as a secondary mission during combat.

2. In conclusion it is contended that soldiers prefer dance music to formal band music and that an available "pick up" orchestra, even though not highly proficient, is preferable to the occasional appearance of a formal band.

FOR	AGAINST
21	50

APPENDIX NO. 2

Administration — Infantry Division

THE INFANTRY CONFERENCE

FORT BENNING, GEORGIA

R E P O R T O F C O M M I T T E E

O N O R G A N I Z A T I O N

SHORT TITLE

ADMINISTRATION -- INFANTRY DIVISION

(O-8)

PRIORITY NUMBER

(13)

June 1946

ORGANIZATION OF THE COMMITTEE

Brigadier General Frederick Mc Cabe	Chairman
Colonel William W. O'Connor, INF	Secretary
Major John McWatters, INF	Asst Secretary

SUB-COMMITTEE PREPARING THE REPORT

Colonel J.A. Dabney, Infantry	Chairman
Lieutenant Colonel W.C. Chapman, Infantry	Member
Lieutenant Colonel Carlyle F. McDannel, Infantry	Member
Major George S. Beatty Jr., Infantry	Member

OTHER COMMITTEE MEMBERS

Colonel H.W. Zwicker, GSC (Infantry)

Colonel M.J. Young, (Engineers)

Colonel J.T. O'Neill, (Engineers)

Colonel R.J. Meyer, (Signal Corps)

Colonel Vennard Wilson, (Cavalry)

Colonel B.A. Byrne, (Infantry)

Lieutenant Colonel Frank S. Holcombe, (Infantry)

Lieutenant Colonel D.A. King, (Field Artillery)

Lieutenant Colonel G.A. Nida, (Ordanance)

Lieutenant Colonel W.M. Summers, (Infantry)

Lieutenant Colonel John Williamson, (Infantry)

Lieutenant Colonel Ellis W. Williamson, (Infantry)

Lieutenant Colonel E.D. Van Alstyne, (Infantry)

Major Herbert F. Crecelius, (Chemical Warfare Service)

Major Lawson E. Hahn, (Infantry)

Major William H. Lynch Jr., (Infantry)

Major Edward W. McGregor, (Infantry)

Major Hunter M. Montgomery, (Infantry)

TABULATION OF COMMITTEE VOTE

O-8 Administration - Infantry Division   RECOMMENDATIONS

	No. 1		No. 2		No. 3	
	Yes	No	Yes	No	Yes	No
Brig. Gen. F. Mc Cabe	X		X		X	
Col. V. Wilson	X		X		X	
Col. B. A. Byrne	X		X		X	
Col. R. W. Zwicker	X		X		X	
Col. M. J. Young	Officer departed in compliance with orders prior to presentation of stud					
Col. J. T. O'Neill	X		X		X	
Col. R. J. Meyer	X		X		X	
Col. J. A. Dabney	X		X		X	
Lt. Col. J. Williamson	X		X		X	
Lt. Col. E. D. Van Alstyne	X		X		X	
Lt. Col. E. W. Williamson	X		X		X	
Lt. Col. F. S. Holcombe	X		X		X	
Lt. Col. G. A. Nida	X		X		X	
Lt. Col. W. M. Summers	X		X		X	
Lt. Col. D. A. King	X		X		X	
Lt. Col. W. C. Chapman	X		X		X	
Lt. Col. C. F. Mc Dannel	X		X		X	
Major E. W. McGregor	X		X		X	
Major H. M. Montgomery	X		X		X	
Major H. F. Crecelius	Officer sitting and voting with Com Tactics "A" during presentation of this study.					
Major W. R. Lynch Jr.	X		X		X	
Major G. S. Beatty Jr.	X		X		X	
Major L. E. Hahn	X		X		X	
TOTALS	21		21		21	

THE INFANTRY CONFERENCE
FORT BENNING, GEORGIA

14 June 1946

SUBJECT: Short Title: Administration- Infantry Division (O-8)

I. Papers accompanying.

    1. Bibliography (TAB A)

    2. Testimonials (TAB B)

    3. Extracts from Statements (TAB C)

II. The Study Presented.

    How should administration be handled within the Infantry Division during combat, and what organization should be established for this purpose in the rear echelon?

III. Facts Bearing on the Study.

    1. While the destruction of the enemy is at all times the primary objective of the infantry division, it is generally recognized that the "paper war" must go on concurrently.

    2. In combat unit personnel sections are usually at division rear headquarters in an Administrative Center or with the service company of the regiment, depending upon the type of operation the division is involved in.

    3. At present regimental personnel sections are made up of one (1) Captain and one (1) Tech Sgt augmented by the company clerks (with their typewriters) from each company in the regiment. This leaves the company commander without a clerk and without a typewriter.

    4. Personnel sections are most effectively organized when definite groups are assigned definite jobs, such as one group to handle nothing but morning reports, another to handle only payrolls, etc. This does not keep the company clerk qualified in company administration nor does it keep him available to the company commander for work.

    5. Transportation and equipment for unit personnel sections is not now provided by T/O and E.

- 3 -

6. Section II, WD Circular #198, 30 June 1945 authorizes a T/5, mail clerk for companies or similar units but he usually has a full time job delivering and picking up mail and making his reports.

7. Companies have some paper work which it is neither economical nor practical to have the clerk in the personnel section do.

8. The strength of the personnel sections in the infantry division is: 66 for infantry regiments, 29 for division artillery, 5 for special troops excluding Div Hq & Hq Company but including Div Recon. Troop, 6 for Engr Bn, and 10 for Medical Bn. Total 116 officers, warrant officers and enlisted men. Many combat divisions found that they had to have more than this number.

9. When personnel sections are at Div Rear they are usually superimposed on Div Hq Co and additional ratings and equipment are taken from line units to help the Div Hq Co take care of the control, protection and feeding of these men.

IV. Conclusions,

1. Individual companies and batteries need some clerical assistance in combat which it is difficult for them to get under the present set up.

2. Inasmuch as the most efficient use of personnel sections is obtained by sectionalizing work and as the section is normally with the service company or battery or at Div Rear Ech there appears to be no good reason for having the men that do that work assigned to each individual company or battery.

3. The entire unit personnel section should be assigned to the service company or battery of each regt, separate bn, and Hq Spec Troops and designated as clerks in the unit personnel section in the T/O. T/E equipment including tentage, typewriters, etc. should be earmarked for the unit personnel section in the T/O &E.

4. When possible administration within the infantry division during combat should be handled in a Div. Administrative Center located at Div Rear Ech. In the Administrative Center would be

- 4 -

located all unit personnel officers and their sections. This organization should be flexible in order to enable the unit personnel section to revert to regiments or battalions when dispersal demands, as in island warfare or detachment of one regiment.

5. Division Hq Co. should be authorized mess personnel, mess equipment, and vehicles in the T/O & E sufficient to administer this Administrative Center.

6. Div Hq Co. T/O should authorize a field officer designated as Hq. Comdt Div Rear Ech to run the messes, motor park, billeting, etc.

7. Organization of unit personnel sections in the service company or battery of units, leaving company and battery clerks with their company or battery, and augmentation of Div Hq Co to handle the Division Administrative Center would result in an increase of approximately seventy five (75) men to the present Division strength.

V. Recommendations

1. That an organic personnel section, exclusive of company and battery clerks, be established in the service company or battery of each regiment or separate battalion and in Hq Special Troops for special troop units.

2. That wherever possible administration within the Infantry Division during combat be handled in a Division Administration center located at the Division Rear Echelon.

3. That Div Hq Co be augmented in the T/O & E sufficiently to enable it to handle the Division Administrative Center without assistance from the line units.

VI. Concurrences

The committee concurrs in the foregoing conclusions and recommendations.

(s)

FREDERICK MC CABE
Brigadier General USA
Chairman

BIBLIOGRAPHY

TITLE	FILE NO.	DATE
AGF Observer's Report - 2nd Armored Div		12 April 1944
AGF Observer's Report - 82nd Airborne Div		27 March 1944
AGF Observer's Report - 69th Infantry Div		21 October 1944
Theater Notes, ETO		February 1944
AGF Observer's Report - 1st Infantry Div		13 April 1944
Recommended changes in Div Hq T/O	5	
Comments Comdt FA School		28 May 1946
Overseas Experience of Service Units, Hq AGF		31 July 1944
ETO Board Report	5	
37th Div Report		
Organization of G-1 Sec	8	
Division Command Post SOP	Military Review	Aug 1943
Service Areas of the Infantry Division	" "	June 1943
Reduction of Paper Work	" "	April 1943
For First Sergeants only	Infantry Journal	December 1944

TESTIMONIAL

Maj. Gen. Wm. F. Dean, CG 44th Div

    I do not favor any standard organization for the handling of administration in the rear echelon. Each division commander will want to handle it differently and there are many cases where units will be detached and need their own administrative help.

    We used our band at the Forward Echelon for playing units out of the line, guard at the CP, and burial of the dead.

    Our rear echelon was commanded by the Division AG.

TESTIMONIAL

LT COLONEL JOHN J. DEANE, 0185004, AGD

How should administration be handled in the Infantry
Division during combat, and what organization should be established for this purpose in rear echelon: (Title: Administration - Infantry Division)

The following testimony is based on my experience as Ad-
jutant General of the 36th Infantry Division from April 1943 to
October 1944.

1. It is my experience that the following numbers of personnel are usually assigned to the rear echelon while the Infantry
Division is in combat.

	Officers	EM	Total
Infantry Regiments (3)	6	105	111
Division Artillery - 4 Battalions	4	32	36
Headquarters, Special Troops	2	5	7
Special Troops, Personnel Section	1	7	8
Division Surgeon	3	3	6
Inspector	3	3	6
Judge Advocate	2	2	4
Finance	3	17	20
Special Service	1	3	4
Adjutant General - Decoration Section (10)	7	36	43
Chaplain	2	2	4
Headquarters Company			
Company Headquarters	1	10	11
Special Platoon	0	13	13
Transportation Platoon	1	14	15
Band	2	56	58
Engineer Battalion	1	6	7
Tank and T/D Battalion	2	16	18
Strays - Reclass, etc.	5	20	25
	46	350	396

2. The shortages in equipment as shown in the present T/O &
E 7-2 are substantially as follows:

Ranges	3-Unit	3
Tents	Storage	4
Tents	Kitchen - Fly-proof	2
Stoves	N1941 - Tent	8
Heaters	Immersion	6
Typewriters	Non-portable - 12" carriage	21

a. As it stands now, division headquarters company is
authorized three 3-unit ranges for the Infantry troops and one
1-unit range for use of aircraft section. This is not sufficient.
Normally an officer's mess and an enlisted mess are operated in the
combat command post. These messes require a minimum of two 3-unit
ranges. Normally the rear echelon will need three 3-unit ranges;
one set for officers and two sets for enlisted men.

b. The T/O & E does not show any tents, storage. This is the type of tentage normally used by the AG and the Finance Officer. The AG will need three and the Finance Officer one. I am assuming that tentage for the personnel sections will be furnished by parent unit.

c. Two additional tents, kitchen, fly-proof, will be needed for the two 3-unit ranges which I have proposed.

d. The T/O & E authorized nine typewriters, non-portable, 11". These are not entirely satisfactory as they will not accommodate letter size paper turned lengthwise, while a 12" carriage typewriter will do so. I believe the nine 11" carriage typewriters should be eliminated and replaced by twenty-one 12" carriage typewriters. It is my experience that the AG office and other special staff sections were never able to operate on the T/O allowance of typewriters and, consequently, were forced to obtain additional machines by schemes which were sometimes illegal, such as borrowing them from base sections and forgetting to return them. It must be borne in mind that the AG section of a division in combat usually includes a large Decorations subsection which is not shown in the T/O. This section will need about eight typewriters. The other four will be available as a pool for use by the general staff sections or the other special staff sections.

e. The T/O & E provides sixteen heaters, immersion. With the addition of two kitchens, six additional heaters will be required.

3. Command of the Rear Echelon.

a. It is my experience that the rear echelon will run more smoothly if commanded by a line officer of mature age, combat ability, and a good deal of administrative experience.

b. It is possible that this officer may be president of the division general court which will handle many important cases, such as trial under AW 75. To meet this requirement, he should have some legal experience. To avoid friction, he should be senior to the Lt Colonels of the special staff.

c. My experience has shown it to be a great mistake to place a combat cast-off in command of the rear echelon. Such an officer is immediately looked down upon by all concerned from buck privates up, whether he was relieved from combat because of inefficiency or because of lack of courage.

d. As a general rule, the commanding officer of Special Troops can fill this job very nicely provided he is given a reasonable amount of latitude by the division commander and further provided that the division Chief of Staff does not tell him exactly how to do the rear echelon job.

e. The commander of the rear echelon must understand that the operation of the personnel sections and the AG office is the responsibility of the AG and that the enlisted men of those sections must not be harassed by unnecessary formations, training or other useless chores.

4. Handling of Administration in the Division During Combat.

a. The best plan seems to be consolidation of personnel sections of divisional units including those of attached T/D tank or other type battalions in the rear echelon under direct control of division AG.

b. When this arrangement is established, division AG will coordinate the flow of information from all sources to the battle casualty sections concerned. His files will be the clearing house for all types of personnel information. A work-sheet type of morning report will be delivered to the AG section each day from the battle area and other locations by courier. These work-sheet type morning reports are distributed by AG sections to appropriate personnel officers who in turn prepare the typed morning reports. The Graves Registration Officers' reports, the Clearing Companies admission and disposition sheets and those from the adjacent divisions will be on file in the AG office. These records, together with the morning report, constitute the basis on which battle casualty reports are prepared. In normal practice no individual should be reported dead unless the Graves Registration Officer reports he has the body. This was the policy in my division.

c. Normally the post office will not be in the rear echelon but will be set up with the Class I dump. This has been found to be the most satisfactory plan, especially in a fast moving situation. The QM Company Commander furnishes transportation to carry the mail, incoming and outgoing. This is the economy feature that when no mail trucks are needed none are tied up. As a further economy feature, the ration trucks from the organization pick up the mail when they call for rations.

5. Handling of Replacements and Returnees from Hospital.

a. The most satisfactory plan appears to be establishment of an office force of one AG man with the Class I dump. All replacements are routed to this NCO. Messing and shelter is provided by the commanding officer of the QM Company. Hospital returnees will be returned to their former units automatically on ration transportation by the AG NCO. Replacements will be distributed to appropriate units in the same manner according to instructions received from the AG office which will in turn receive them from G-1.

6. Defense.

a. Defense of the rear echelon should be in the hands of the rear echelon commander. The troops to be used are those of the personnel sections plus the thirty to forty men of headquarters company who will normally be in the rear echelon. As shown in tabulation in paragraph 1, the strength of the command will run around forty-six officers and 350 men. The backbone consists of the personnel sections of the three Infantry regiments. A firm chain of command should be laid down. Each officer in the rear echelon should be assigned his specific duty. Any attack on the rear echelon will probably occur without warning, hence sentry and morning arrangements systems must be excellent. Sentries must be carefully trained in the use of the challenge and countersign. In areas where night attacks might occur I believe one platoon should be on alert constantly. The men may be permitted to sleep but should be dressed and should have their arms beside them.

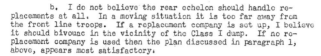

b. I do not believe the rear echelon should handle replacements at all. In a moving situation it is too far away from the front line troops. If a replacement company is set up, I believe it should bivouac in the vicinity of the Class I dump. If no replacement company is used then the plan discussed in paragraph 1, above, appears most satisfactory.

7. The Rear Echelon Headaches.

a. We once had a rear echelon commander who insisted that his staff officers - he had six of them - eat in a mess set up separately one-quarter of a mile distant from the regular rear echelon officers' mess. What this did to cooks, KP's and mess equipment is obvious. His attitude incensed the officers of the special staff. I believe all officers of the rear echelon should eat at one mess.

b. The same rear echelon commander referred to in paragraph 1 set up tents for his six staff officers 1/2 mile away from the rest of the command. This also increased the ill feeling against him. I think all officers in the rear echelon should be bivouaced in the same area.

c. This same commander usually set himself up in a palatial office whenever buildings were available. His office occupied approximately the same amount of floor space as the division AG office which employed forty people. Needless to say, the AG did not like this.

d. Rear echelon commanders should not assemble the special staff for conferences. The need for a general conference is rare. The rear echelon commander referred to in preceding paragraphs frequently assembled the officers of the special staff to hear him orate at great length on matters of little importance. This should be avoided as it kills too much time.

e. The rear echelon commander must be particularly careful with the enlisted men and must insure that enlisted men have a decent place to eat. I have seen the enlisted men of our rear echelon eat in the rain day after day for three straight weeks. The officers had tentage for 1 mess hall.

f. The rear echelon commander should also be particularly careful about the shelter provided for the clerks in the rear echelon. He must understand that they are more delicate than the combat troops up forward and must have protection from the weather. They must also be provided with the best available office space. Buildings may be available, if not, tents should be pitched in places which will provide natural light in daytime and will permit being blacked out at night so work can go on.

g. The rear echelon commander must understand that the personnel of the AG section and the personnel clerks and the JA and Finance Officer have a primary mission other than fighting or training. They must not be harassed by work details or defense details except in emergency.

h. Any training which is given the rear echelon must be timely. I remember one of our rear echelon commanders having an hour of training each day devoted to anti-aircraft defense at a time when the Luftwaffe was practically nonexistent. This same commander also scheduled three hour road marches three times a week. These long marches broke the work day for clerks completely.

JOHN J. DEANE
Lt Colonel, AGD
Hq, The Inf School

- 11 -

THE INFANTRY CONFERENCE

FORT BENNING, GEORGIA

8 June 1946

REFERENCE:

Extract of T/Os showing Personnel of an Infantry Division who normally operate in the Rear Echelon During Combat

	Officers:	EM:	Total:
Infantry Regiments (Personnel Section – Each Regiment – 1 O & 23 EM)	3	69	72
Division Artillery	1 (WO)	20	21
Division Headquarters Company	0	37	37
Headquarters, Special Troops		1	1
M.P. Co		1	1
Ordnance Co		1	1
Signal Co		1	1
Cav Rcn Troop		1	1
Med Bn	3	3	6
Eng Bn		4	4
Band	2 (WO)	56	58
Division Headquarters		4	4
I.G.	3 (1-WO)	3	6
J.A.G.	2 (1-WO)	2	4
Public Relations	1	10	11
Finance	3 (1-WO)	17	20
Special Service	1	3	4
A.G.	8 (3-WO)	40	48
Chem		2	2
Chaplain	2	—	2
Totals--	29	275	304

NOTES:-

1. For each attached TD, TK and AA Bn, there will be 1 <u>off</u> and 8 <u>EM</u> normally attached to Div Rr Ech, AG Section.

2. Information based on combat experiences evidenced that each Regimental Personnel Section usually had <u>2 off</u> and <u>35 EM</u> working in the rear echelon instead of the figures shown above.

3. The strength of the personnel working in the rear echelon from the Separate Bns, Engr, Med, Art, etc., likewise was increased by several clerks.

Tab C

APPENDIX NO. 1   21 June 1946

CONFERENCE DISCUSSION

COMMITTEE REPORT PRESENTED

O-8 How should administration be handled within the
infantry division during combat, and what organization should
be established for this purpose in rear echelon?

NO DISCUSSION

APPENDIX NO. 1

THE INFANTRY CONFERENCE
FORT BENNING, GEORGIA

21 June 1946

COMPILATION OF CONFERENCE VOTE

QUESTION: C-8 "How should administration be handled within
the Infantry Division during combat, and what organization should be established for this purpose in the rear
echelon?"

RECOMMENDATIONS:

1. That an organic personnel section, exclusive of
   company and battery clerks, be established in the
   service company or battery of each regiment or
   separate battalion and in Hq Special Troops for
   special troop units.

   110 FOR   0   AGAINST

2. That wherever possible administration within the
   Infantry Division during combat be handled in a
   Division Administration Center located at the
   Division Rear Echelon.

   109 FOR   1   AGAINST

3. That Div Hq Co be augmented in the T/C & E
   sufficiently to enable it to handle the Division
   Administrative Center without assistance from the
   line units.

   110 FOR   0   AGAINST

WRITTEN COMMENTS

Lt. Col. J. J. Stovall: Yes to committee recommendation 1, excepting the Section should be placed with
the headquarters company and not with the service
company.

APPENDIX NO. 2

CPSIA information can be obtained at www.ICGtesting.com
Printed in the USA
BVOW10s1428270114

343141BV00011B/955/P

9 781288 5879